WHAT PEOPL

TREES OF

T0167564

A beautiful tribute to the nature beings that refresh our Planet and our spirit, *Trees of the Goddess* is a portal to deep feminine wisdom ways – a guidebook that will make the mystery and magic of trees come alive for all who read.
Llyn Roberts, MA, author of *The Good Remembering, Shamanic Reiki* and *Shapeshifting into Higher Consciousness* LlynRoberts.com and eomec.org

Elen Sentier has encompassed the knowledge and wisdom of our beautiful trees in this wonderful book. Fascinating information not only on the magic of trees but how they intertwine with the universe, how we can work with them and what amazing sources of information, inspiration and guidance they can be. This book goes far beyond the structure of Ogham and takes the reader on a spiritual journey through the forest of the Goddess.
Rachel Patterson, author of *A Kitchen Witch's World of Magical Herbs & Plants, Grimoire of a Kitchen Witch, Pagan Portals - Hoodoo, Pagan Portals - Kitchen Witchcraft* and *Pagan Portals - Moon Magic*

Any book by Elen Sentier will reflect her very individual yet spiritual approach to the subject and will include her specialised knowledge and intuition. She has been a teacher of Ogham for many years and knows what she is talking about so a book about this written by her will be both authoritative in the truth of the information in it and educational in the true sense of the word!
Steve Andrews, author of *Herbs of the Northern Shaman*

Shaman Pathways

Trees of the
Goddess

Shaman Pathways

Trees of the Goddess

Elen Sentier

MOON
BOOKS

Winchester, UK
Washington, USA

First published by Moon Books, 2014
Moon Books is an imprint of John Hunt Publishing Ltd., Laurel House, Station Approach,
Alresford, Hants, SO24 9JH, UK
office1@jhpbooks.net
www.johnhuntpublishing.com
www.moon-books.net

For distributor details and how to order please visit the 'Ordering' section on our website.

Text copyright: Elen Sentier 2013

ISBN: 978 1 78279 332 8

A CIP catalogue record for this book is available from the British Library.

Design: Stuart Davies
Cover: Detail from a painting by Stuart Davies
www.stuartdaviesart.com

Printed and bound by CPI Group (UK) Ltd, Croydon, CR0 4YY

We operate a distinctive and ethical publishing philosophy in all
areas of our business, from our global network of authors to
production and worldwide distribution.

CONTENTS

Tree Magic   1
Sun & Moon Cycles   3

1st Month – A: Ailm: *Scots Pine* & B: Beith: *Birch*   7
2nd Month – L: Luis: *Rowan*   16
3rd Month – N: Nuin: *Ash*   19
4th Month – O – Onn: *Furze* & F: Fearn: *Alder*   22
5th Month – S: Saille: *Willow*   29
6th Month – S/Z: Straif *Blackthorn* & H: Uath *Hawthorn*   34
7th Month – U – Ura: *Heather* & D: Duir: *Oak*   42
8th Month – T: Tinne: *Holly*   52
9th Month – C: Coll: *Hazel* & Q: Quert: *Apple*   56
10th Month – E – Eadha: *Poplar* & M: Muin: *Bramble*   63
11th Month – G: Gort: *Ivy*   72
12th Month – I: Iolo: *Yew* & P/B: Peith: *Guelder Rose*   74
13th Month – R: Ruis: *Elder*   82

Mistletoe   85
Ways to work with the Trees   88
Moon Bath   91
Allies ...   94
Making your Ogham Staves   97
Spirit Keeping   100

Tree Magic

Jung said ... *Trees in particular were mysterious, and seemed to me direct embodiments of the incomprehensible meaning of life. For that reason, the woods were the place that I felt closest to its deepest meaning and to its awe-inspiring workings.*
Jung (1995, 86).

This was my experience too. Now it all seems as if it was long ago and faraway ... but it wasn't. Not long ago at all for I am only 65. It wasn't far away either but here in this wonderful land of Britain where people still know and understand the trees. It happened at places called Nymet and Nympton which are Devonshire words for *nemeton*, a sacred space. My uncle was one of the wise and cunning folk of the Devon villages where I grew up and, along with the other elders and wise folk, told me of the trees and of the goddess.

All this takes me back into old memories and time-travel journeys in which I revisit childhood haunts and it's all still here, still with us, today.

There are twenty British trees that work very comfortably with the goddess and link to humankind. Over the ages people have brought them together in what we know as the ogham. Some say they are just an alphabet, a means of writing, but they are far more than that and far older, too, than many give them credit for.

The spirits of the trees of the goddess still live in the woods and they will speak with us, show us things, take us on journeys, if we ask. The goddess will help us to find the old ways that our elders knew ... the ways where reality is huge and exciting rather than small and frightening. I offer you the gifts that were given to me all those years ago.

The trees will speak to you, they will draw the kenning out of

I

you. To walk in the deer-trods of the goddess all you have to do is ask ...

Sun & Moon Cycles

Here on earth, we work with the cycles of the sun, the star which gives us light and warmth, which enables life. And we work with the moon which reflects the light of the sun down onto the earth in the hours of darkness when the sun cannot be seen directly.

The **sun-cycle** is about the four changes in the sun's arc that define the seasons of our year –

- Midwinter solstice
- Spring equinox
- Midsummer solstice
- Autumn equinox.

To these four the goddess adds a fifth feast, the time of Samhain which is the threshold, the doorway, between the old year and the new in our tradition. The watchwords of these five feasts are the last verse of the Song of Amergin in which the bard tells how he is and has been everything. It begins with *I am a stag of seven tines…* and finishes with these five lines …

I am the womb of every holt
I am the blaze on every hill
I am the queen of every hive
I am the shield to every head
I am the tomb to every hope
(Song of Amergin translated by Robert Graves, from The White Goddess, Faber and Faber Limited, 24 Russell Square The London WC1. It appears here under the principle of Fair Use.)

As ever with the Celts, it's a riddle-poem and it takes work to tease out what the goddess is showing us.

Vowel Sounds

These five lines also relate to the five sacred trees that hold the vowel sounds. Vowels are sounds we make without obstructing the breath with our tongue, teeth or lips; the air comes out from our lungs without any hindrance and is shaped only by our mouths. The vowels are about the air, spirit, coming straight through you and their sounds are held by the four sun-feasts and Samhain.

Each of the five feasts expresses an aspect of the goddess ...

I am the womb of every holt	A – Ailm: Scots pine who holds midwinter
I am the blaze on every hill	O – Onn: Furze who carries spring equinox
I am the queen of every hive	U – Ura: Heather who holds midsummer
I am the shield to every head	E – Eadha: Poplar who carries the autumn equinox
I am the tomb to every hope	I – Iolo: Yew who holds Samhain

The Consonants

Consonants work differently. Unlike the vowels, the consonants work by the air passing *through* or *across* some sort of barrier formed by the tongue, teeth and/or lips *as well as* being shaped by the mouth. This is significant for breath-spirit ... it means you get quite involved with the production of the sound, beyond allowing the air to pass through your vocal cords. They are about how you *form* and *inform* the air as it passes through you ... this is a big responsibility.

The 13 moon-months work with the sacred trees that hold the sounds of the consonants in the tree alphabet. The 6th and 9th months are held by two trees that work together.

The consonant moon-months begin with Beith, Birch, at the

time of the midwinter solstice and run alongside the five feasts of the goddess. The 5 vowel trees each work with one of the consonant trees at their seasons.

Moon Cycles

These five feasts are again reflected by the moon as her four major quarters – new, 1st quarter, full and 3rd quarter hold the first four feasts while Samhain is held by the waning crescent moon.

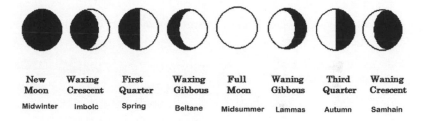

New Moon	Waxing Crescent	First Quarter	Waxing Gibbous	Full Moon	Waning Gibbous	Third Quarter	Waning Crescent
Midwinter	Imbolc	Spring	Beltane	Midsummer	Lammas	Autumn	Samhain

These are the 8 phases of the moon. They also reflect the 8 seasons in the Celtic year. The moon reflects the sun's annual cycle; they dance together. This reminds us of how these cycles enable us to live; they show us that the cycles work in both *little* (over each month) and in *large* (over the year).

How is it these cycles work?

The new moon happens when the moon is between the earth and sun. The three are in alignment so the entire illuminated portion of the moon is on the back side of the moon, the part we cannot see. Hence we have the name "Dark Moon".

At a full moon, the earth, moon, and sun are again aligned but this time the moon is on the opposite side of the earth, so the entire sunlit part of the moon is facing us.

Both the first and third quarter moons are often called a half moon because we see a semicircle of lighted moon. This happens because the moon is at a 90 degree angle with respect to the earth and sun.

At the times of the crescent moons is she is at a 45 degree

5

angle to the earth so we see the beautiful thin sickle-shape that is so evocative. If the crescent sits in your cupped right hand it's waxing, if it sits in your cupped left hand then it's waning. Waxing means growing while waning means shrinking.

At the time of the gibbous moons she is at an angle of 135 degrees so we see a wide belly of moonlight cut by a sliver of darkness. The word *month* comes from the word *moon*; it is about the cycles of the moon. The moon cycles through visibility, light, life, every 28 days. She shows us the cycle of birth, culmination, death and rebirth 13 times every year.

A good way to get this knowing into your noggin is the following exercise. Hold a ball and sit in a swivel chair with a desk light pointing at you; the light is the sun, the ball is the moon and you are the earth. Watch the light on the ball as you swivel round, you'll see the effects as in the diagram of the moon phases.

We've been using this moon-system of counting days and seasons for a very long time. Palaeolithic tally sticks show that our ancestors counted the days in relation to the moon's phases and many peoples still base their calendars on the moon. Nowadays the modern world works on a year of 365.25 days divided into 12 months; this is now the international calendar. It was introduced by Pope Gregory XIII in 1582 to sort out the leapyear problems of the calendar Julius Caesar introduced in 45 BC. The moon calendar is far, far older than either of these and connects us intimately with the natural seasons of our solar system.

1st Month – A: Ailm: *Scots Pine* & B: Beith: *Birch*

A: Ailm: Scots Pine

Ailm, Scots pine, is the first of the five feasts of the goddess.

Time: Sun-return

Watchwords: *I am the womb of every holt*

Metal: Silver

Planet: Moon

Concept: Rebirth

Ailm represents our letter **A**

The Scots pine (*Pinus sylvestris*) is a very ancient tree ... as befits the beginning-tree for the ogham. Scots pine is about breaking up land to become earth and soil and support growing things. It is an initiator of change; breaking up old things so that new can grow ... this is rebirth.

The Scots pine is native to Europe and Asia, ranging to the Caucasus Mountains in the south and as far north as inside the Arctic Circle; all around the realm of the Boreal Forest. It formed large parts of forests in Great Britain, particularly in the north of England and in Scotland, until 8,000 years ago. Pollen records show it spread to the British Isles after the Ice Age 9,000 years ago and spread across Britain, possibly from Scandinavia via "Doggerland". Eight-thousand years ago the ice melted and the sea levels rose so Britain became separated from Europe. Then, between 4,000 and 1,500 years ago, the Irish and west Scottish pines declined massively and the Irish pines went extinct. This may be why the silver fir was taken as the tree for Ailm by the Irish when they further developed the ogham in the early middle ages. In Britain Scots pine is now natural only in Scotland. Scots pine went extinct in Wales and England due to over-exploitation and grazing 3-400 years ago but is now being re-introduced.

The oldest known Scots pine blew down at Inveraray in 1951 and was thought to be over 330 years old. Scots pines are the native pinewoods of Scotland and extremely important for national and international wildlife conservation. Only remnants of the original ancient forests exist as many were burnt for fuel, cleared for farming or overgrazed by sheep and deer after the wolves were gone. Today a long term project is underway working to protect and restore the remnants of the huge ancient forest e.g. Glen Affric, N. Scotland.

The Scots pine is excellent for wildlife supporting lichens and insects. Siskin, great spotted woodpecker, great crested tit and crossbill feed well around them and, in Scotland, wryneck and capercaille live in pinewoods. The level branches are good nesting places for golden eagle, osprey and goshawk, and red squirrels love their cones and seeds.

The tree has fairly short, blue-green needles and orange-red bark; its wood goes from pale to quite dark reddish brown. It was used for making tar in the pre-industrial age and has also been a source of rosin and turpentine. It makes excellent soap and the resin, called pitch pine or fatwood, is a very good fire-starter.

Time: Sun-Return

This is the winter solstice, the longest night and the shortest day of the year. The word solstice means standstill because for three days it appears that the sun rises on the same point on the horizon. This same effect occurs again at midsummer.

The two solstices are significant as they mark times when the year changes from one cycle to another. Our ancestors knew and worked with this. The still common idea that ancient people were frightened the sun might never return is rubbish. People who could put up temples of such superb accuracy as Stonehenge and the many other circles and standing stones were very astute mathematicians who observed the skies. There are very few construction companies who could do as well now, even with all our modern computers and equipment. Our ancestors were extremely intelligent people. It's well worth bearing this in mind as you work through the ogham.

Watchwords

The watchwords for Scots pine, Ailm, are …

- *I am the womb of every holt*

Let's look at the word **womb** – what is the womb? What does it do?

Think about how the seed falls into the womb from the ovary – each month for humans, or at the relevant season for other mammals. The spark of life enters the womb and fertilises the seed. The seed then grows within the darkness to finally birth out into the light.

The *return of the sun* is what ailm is about – in every sense. Every plant, planet, star, animal, human, building, country, nation, idea, book, painting, each journey you make in the everyday world, everything … yes, everything … goes through the birth-death cycle, the cycle of return. Ailm holds this energy for the earth and all her creatures, including us. In Britain this principle is held by the Scots pine.

So what is a **holt**? What does it do?

The word holt means both an otter's den and also a small wood. Both are places of shelter and concealment, a safe place, a nemeton.

The word otter derives from the Old English word *otor* or *oter* which stems from the Proto-Indo-European language root *wódʎ* This gave rise to the English word *water*. The otter's holt is the place by the water where she gives birth and rears her younglings. It is a womb.

Otters are water-and-land creatures, beautiful to watch, supple, graceful and playful. River otters usually only go into the water to hunt or travel, spending a lot of their time on land to avoid their fur becoming waterlogged. Sea otter fur is adapted to enable them to live in the ocean for most of their lives but come ashore to their holt to birth their kits. All otters walk between the worlds of water and earth … this is something they will teach us if we ask.

The womb-holt is a birthing and re-birthing place for us too, leading us between the elements of earth and water, the body-sensing and the feeling functions. Ailm, the goddess and the otter will show us the way.

Metal: Silver

Silver is one of the magical metals. It possesses the highest electrical conductivity of any element and the highest thermal conductivity of any metal. It is malleable, soft and relatively easy to form into shapes. Its chemical symbol, Ag, comes from the Greek *árguros* and the Latin *argentum*, both stem from the Indo-European root *arg* which means grey or shining and are related to *arian*, the Welsh for silver.

In European folklore, silver is a mystical element, a trans-mitter between the worlds. It is associated with the moon. Polished, it has a mirror-surface that reflects back to us as the moon reflects the light of the sun and so is used to make scrying mirrors. It is used to transform water into a healing potion and, in modern times, silver has been shown to have antibacterial properties too. The Silver Branch, Taliesin's calling branch with which he calls to otherworld for inspiration, is a branch of silver bells. The midwinter form of the silver branch is the mistletoe which we still use as part of the red-white-black berry decoration for the midwinter feast. Mistletoe and the moon have always had a connection.

Planet: Moon

The moon has a tremendous effect on the earth; lots of things would go horribly wrong if she wasn't there including that the earth would wobble so badly we would all fall to pieces. We mostly notice how she affects water in the form of tides in the oceans and seas; but we often forget that we, as human beings, are 70% water ... so the moon affects us deeply even if we're not conscious of it.

Women's menstrual cycles, goddess tides, conform closely with the cycle of the moon. Plants and soil creatures are also strongly affected by the moon and their growth – like the rising of sap or the movement of earthworms – corresponds to the moon-cycles.

These cycles, rising and falling, growing and retreating, are about the cycle of the Year and of life itself ... about birth, death and rebirth. Ailm teaches us this.

Concept: Rebirth

The concept of rebirth is fundamental in all the ancient traditions. Our ancestors knew the reality of this and did not think of or fear death in the way most folk do nowadays but knew it as part of the eternal cycle.

Mountains rise up because of geological processes and are then worn down again by weather. Tectonic plates move again and more mountains are created. Trees and plants sprout from the seed, they grow up tall, flower and fruit, then they die back down giving themselves back to the earth only to grow up again. Animals – including human animals – are born, live their lives and then die giving back their atoms to the earth.

The spirit goes on, passing through many incarnations in all sorts of forms, time after time. All life is *animated*, en-spirited. The word comes from the Latin *anima* which derives from an Indo-European root meaning "to breathe". The English word *spirit* comes from the Latin *spiritus* which also means breath. The Latin word comes from a Proto-Indo-European word *(s)peis* which again means breath. Breath is essential for all life.

The spirit is reborn in a new body at the end/beginning of each cycle ... each day, each moon-cycle (month), each sun-cycle, each turning of the year. Our ancestors knew this even more intimately than we do.

As Bob Toben says, in Space-Time and Beyond, *"Death is just a change of cosmic address ... "*

B: Beith: *Birch*

Time: 25 Dec – 20 Jan: Sun-return
Concept: Birch is the tree of *birth*
Beith represents our letter **B**

⊢

Birch, *Betula pendula*, is another ancient and ground-breaking tree. Its common name, *birch*, comes from an old Germanic root, *birka* which has the Proto-Indo-European root *bherəg* meaning *white, bright, to shine*. The rune *berkana* is named for the birch. Birch is found and used by all the people of the Boreal Forest.

Extracts of birch are used for flavouring, for leather oil and in soap and shampoo. Birch-tar, extracted from birch bark, is thermoplastic and waterproof; it was used as glue on arrows and other things as well as for medicinal purposes. Birch leaves are used to make diuretic tea and extracts are used for dyes. Ground up birch bark fermented in sea water is used for seasoning the woollen, hemp or linen sails and the hemp rope of traditional Norwegian boats.

Birch bark has long, horizontal lenticels which separate into thin, papery plates; they've been used for millennia to make cooking/eating pots, boxes, canoes. It's also been used as paper for writing and drawing and it's possible its name, birch, may also have connections with the Sanskrit word *bhurga* which means *a tree whose bark is used for writing upon*. Birch bark, like all paper products, rots down over time, quicker or slower depending on climatic conditions, there is no reason why it should have survived for us to read and every reason to believe our ancient ancestors would have used it. Absence of evidence is *not* evidence of absence!

Birch has a high calorific value (the ability to make heat) as it contains resinous oil; this makes it excellent fire tinder and firewood. It burns without popping, even when frozen or freshly hewn. The bark burns very well even when wet because of the oils. With care, it can be split and scraped into very thin sheets and dust that will ignite from even the smallest of sparks including the low-heat orange sparks from a flint-and-steel. Birch wood is also good for smoking foods and has been used for such for millennia.

Birch sap is a traditional drink for all the Boreal Forest peoples. In Britain it's used to make a delicious wine and also syrup which, like maple syrup, is good on pancakes and waffles.

In healing terms and the folk medicine of many countries, birch simples were used as curative and preventative tonics as well as on the skin in ointments and oils. Boiled and mashed until very soft, birch bark is used for bruises, wounds and cuts. Its astringent leaves can be used as a tisane or tea which is laxative and diuretic, good for clearing out the system … preparatory to new beginnings (see concept below). Modern herbalists use it to help get rid of bacteria that result in cystitis and infections of the urinary tract. The tea and the sap drinks are high in Vitamin C. Soaking the bark in hot water and laying on painful and aching muscles also works. Birch bark oil is antiseptic and helps heal skin wounds or infections like herpes as well as eczema and psoriasis. Modern science is currently investigating betulin, which comes from the bark, as a treatment for skin cancers.

Concept: Beginnings

Birch is the tree of *beginnings*. Birch is a Pioneer Tree, one who begins the re-colonisation of woodlands which has somehow been destroyed.

Beginnings are times of initiating things and setting events in motion, creation, and especially activation. Its time, moon month, is over the period of the midwinter and sun-return, the longest night and the turn-around time from when there is more and more light each day until midsummer. This is how the earth does her new beginnings, setting again in motion the cycle of the year.

The poet Coleridge called birch the Lady of the Woods and birch is one of Elen's special trees. Fly agaric often grows around the roots of birch and fly agaric is the reindeer magic. Northern shamans drink the pee after reindeer have eaten the fly agaric and transmuted its poison through their own bodies. They can then give the pee to their people so the folk can share in the journeys.

Birch has always had associations with fertility; for instance, Scottish Highland folklore tells that if a barren cow is herded with a birch stick she will become fertile, and a pregnant cow so herded will bear a healthy calf.

Birch is also known as the White Lady – one of the titles of Ceridwen whose totem is also the white sow. Ceridwen is a creator/destroyer goddess, one of the fundamental builders of all the universe. Ceridwen, in her maiden-form, is a beautiful woman, clothed in silvery-white with long golden hair. If you look at the birch tree in autumn when the leaves have turned you will see this, the beautiful, graceful, slender white stem crowned by the delicate golden leaves.

2nd Month – L: Luis: *Rowan*

Time: 21 Jan – 17 Feb: Imbolc
Concept: Rowan is the tree of *thresholds* and *gateways*
Luis represents our letter **L**

╠

L; Luis: Rowan

The rowan tree, also known as *quicken* and *mountain ash* in the Welsh Marches where I live, is a well-known magical tree. Quickbeam is its name in much of the British countryside – remember Quickbeam, the Ent, in Lord of the Rings? He is mountain ash. The name rowan may come from the old Norse *Runa* meaning a charm. Rowan's other folk names include rune tree, quickenwood, quickbane, sorbapple, witchenwood, witchbane.

Rowan is a true native in the rocky habitats of Wales and Scotland but has been introduced throughout the country over many hundreds of years. It is a small, quite short-lived tree that often doesn't get much above 15 metres; it can withstand poor soil and icy temperatures, is quite happy in peaty, acidic soil and often seen growing by rocky streams on the high moors and mountains. Rowan loves light and space so, when not on the moors, you may find it at woodland edges rather than in the middle of old woodlands where it would be overshadowed by the big forest trees.

Rowan berries are high in Vitamin C content. They contain ascorbic acid, making them very astringent and are best prepared into jellies or syrups, where the pulp and seeds are strained out, as the seeds and possibly the leaves are known to contain some toxic properties of the kind associated with prussic acid. Fresh juice from the berries was used as a gargle as well as a mild laxative while both jelly and syrup were prescribed for gout. The unripe berries were only used externally, as lotions and on poultices. The fresh flowers were used in an infusion to help kidney disease. Modern herbalists use a tea made from the dried and ground bark and the dried flowers to help with digestive problems and common stomach disorders. This tea was also once thought to cleanse the blood. In Scotland a strong spirit was made by distillation, probably just for drinking.

Rowan berries have a tiny five pointed star (pentagram) on them opposite the stalk and their red colour, as the colour of lordship, is protective. From Scotland to Cornwall equal-armed crosses – symbolising the four elements – are still made from rowan twigs and bound with red thread. They're carried as talismans. Wood used for making talismans is cut on "St Helen's Day" … Helen is the Christianised form of our ancient deer-goddess, Elen.

Concept: Thresholds & Gateways

Rowans are sometimes found growing out of the stumps of other trees or even out of their boughs, or out of an inaccessible cleft in a rock, so not in the ground at all and are known as flying or journey trees. They are *thresholds* between the worlds.

Rowan is the tree of *coming-and-going* … it holds our thresholds and gateways. All thresholds go both ways. What does this mean?

- Threshold is a place of *both* INGRESS (the way in) and EGRESS (the way out).

To *go* anywhere you must also *leave* where you are …

Rowan is a portal, threshold tree offering you the chance of *going* somewhere … and of *leaving* somewhere. Gateways always do this, even if they are only as apparently simple as the gate between your garden and the street, or the front door of your house.

When we are born, we cross the threshold between otherworld and thisworld... from death-to-otherworld which is birth into thisworld, and death-to-thisworld which is birth into otherworld. When we die we cross the threshold between thisworld and otherworld. We go both ways. It's called quickening ... and the quicken tree helps us understand this and learn to do it well.

In order to cross a threshold we often have to give something. Birth and death are like this. Our spirit inhabits this body which is made of earth-stuff, goddess stuff, for the duration of each incarnation – the body is a space-suit for living on planet earth. The goddess is the earth in the Celtic tradition and everything our bodies are made of comes from her; it all must go back to her when our bodies die. We are both spirit *and* matter while we live on the earth. We give this matter back to the earth at the end of the incarnation when our spirit no longer needs it. Rowan holds this threshold for us.

In Scotland kings were crowned by or under a rowan tree, and all important decisions were made there too. Rowan stands at the threshold between worlds, connecting above, below, north, east, south and west, and within – the seven directions that hold the interface. One of these threshold rowan trees stood on the Orkney Islands and it was said that if even one leaf was carried away from the island, the Orkneys would pass under foreign dominion.

3rd Month – N: Nuin: *Ash*

Time: 18 Feb – 17 Mar
Concept: Ash is a tree of *shifting*
Nuin represents our letter **N**

N: Nuin: Ash

Ash, *Fraxinus excelsior,* is the third most common tree species in Britain; its seedlings root anywhere for a pastime and are often called weeds (i.e. plant in the wrong place from the human perspective) and so become the dominant tree in a wood. It is found across the lands of the Boreal Forest.

The tree's common name, ash, goes back to the Old English *æsc* while its biological name, fraxinus, originated in Latin. Both words mean *spear* which is very appropriate to Gwydion and his story as you'll see later.

Ash has long, finger-like leaves and its buds look like black fingernails; its seeds are known as keys. Rowans or mountain ashes are *not* related to *fraxinus* but belong to the genus *sorbus*. People can confuse the two trees until they get experienced as the leaves and buds are superficially similar.

Ash wood is strong and flexible. The Anglo-Saxons used it for their spears and shield-handles. Nowadays it's used for tool handles, furniture, sports equipment, walking sticks, tent pegs, oars, gates, wheel rims. In World War II ash was used on the aircraft wings of the De Havilland Mosquito. In Wales and Ireland all oars and coracle slats are made of ash to protect against drowning.

Now, in the early years of the twenty-first century, ash is

subject to the ash die-back disease which threatens to wipe it out in Britain and Europe. We must hope that some trees will pull through and so repopulate our forests.

Concept: Shifting

Ash is Gwydion's tree in the British tradition and Gwydion is the master enchanter of all Britain. He is also the master shapeshifter.

His story, with his nephew/son Llew, focuses around a spear, the spear Gronw makes to kill Llew, to transport him into his totem Eagle so he can grow from a boy into a king. The ash spear is a form of transmutation, a changing of the essence rather than just the outer form and this is a very deep form of shapeshifting. It is a creator/destroyer tree, a tree that carries the essence of "power" – the life-spark. This is somewhat echoed in the Scandinavian tradition where ash is the World Tree, Yggdrasil, and the Tree of Rebirth and Healing.

Shapeshifting is one of the most alluring and fascinating of the shamanic skills ... it's also one of the most dangerous. It's very easy to become entranced in the form of something else and unable to return to one's own form, as happens to Llew in the story.

Shapeshifting can be ...

- TRANSFORMATION – changing one's *form*, rather like changing one's clothes, and/or
- TRANSMUTATION – changing one's *essence*.

We all shapeshift, if only when we wear a suit to work and jeans to play! Shapeshifting can be as simple as that. It may be much more, such as taking on the form of another creature or plant or rock, twining one's spirit with another creature, or it may be transmuting one's essence into a whole new being. This last is often imaged through the change a caterpillar makes to become a butterfly.

It's important to understand these aspects of shapeshifting – so you know *what* you are doing, and *when*, and *for what* purpose.

Shapeshifting is about *being appropriate* to one's company, the time and place one is in, and (of course) to one's spirit. To be able to communicate well with others we need to be able to do all of these things at the drop of a hat, to be in the right place, at the right time, in the right shape.

Gwydion is the master enchanter of Britain and a master shifter as his stories tell us. There are times in these stories when we might well think he is being inappropriate to say the least! But I'm never convinced about this. Things happen that (in modern life) we are encouraged to think of as being quite out of place ... but are they? If Gwydion hadn't done what he did would the rest of the story have been able to happen? Being appropriate is *not* about being normal, conforming, doing things that others approve of; it's far more often about upsetting apple-carts ... which Gwydion does very well.

Gwydion is The Trickster and feared by those who don't have a very wide or deep perspective. As you walk this path you come to realise that Tricksters are the very best of Teachers and Friends who will really and truly help you to grow ... if you're up for it.

Gwydion and Nuin are our masters in the skill of shifting.

4th Month – O – Onn: *Furze* & F: Fearn: *Alder*

O: Onn: *Furze*
Time: Spring equinox
Watchwords: *I am the blaze on every hill*
Metal: Gold
Planet: Sun
Concept: Initiation
Onn represents our letter **O**

Onn, Furze, is the second of the five feasts of the goddess.

Furze, Gorse or Whin

Gorse, *Ulex europaeus*, is a fire plant. It is beautifully adapted to both encourage and work with fire. It's highly flammable and its seed pods are opened by fire so it regenerates rapidly after fire. The burnt stumps sprout readily too. If the land it grows in doesn't experience fire then the furze is soon shaded out by taller-growing plants. Regular *swaling* (controlled burning) on moors like Exmoor and Dartmoor helps the gorse to grow well.

Furze is of the pea family. It likes sunny sites with dry, sandy soils, and is found all up the west coast of Europe. The flowers are beautiful, bright golden and honey-scented. It first comes into flower in late summer and autumn, goes on through the winter then it makes a great burst of gold in spring, around or soon after the equinox. Being a pea, it has good nitrogen-fixing qualities – it's been used for land reclamation like mine tailings – and so helps other plants establish better.

It's a wonderful wildlife plant giving dense thorny cover to protect the nests of birds like the Dartford Warbler and European Stonechat. The common name of the Whinchat comes from the bird's living in the *whin* – another name for gorse. The flowers and the dry wood are food for several moth caterpillars. It's also winter food for the feral Exmoor ponies.

Gorse flowers are edible, good in salads, tea and make a lovely flower wine. As it's highly flammable, bundles of gorse were used to fire up traditional bread ovens. Its wood is used in carving. Gorse is one of the Bach flower remedies, used to enable hope in cases where the patient feels all hope has been lost. Gardeners use the gorse remedy to encourage limp plant cuttings to take root.

Time – Spring Equinox

Equinoxes are the other half of the solstices; the times when there are *equal hours* of light and dark. The vernal equinox, as it's called in astronomy, is the real beginning of spring. For the previous six months of the year there has been more darkness than light each day. Now, for the next six months, there will be more light than dark.

Each day the light grows, giving everything hope. Plants grow fast and animals too. In nature many animals give birth to their young around this time to coincide with this big flush of plant growth and the lush plants are food for insects and birds as well as grazers. This, in turn, helps the carnivores who also need food for themselves and their young. In our hunter-gatherer days we too followed this cycle.

Watchwords

The watchwords for Onn, Furze, are

- *I am the blaze on every hill*

Blaze means to burn fiercely or brightly. As a fire plant, as well as from its wonderful golden flowering at springtime gorse, is indeed a "blaze". Furze is about instigating, initiating, pioneering and breaking new ground – all the things the fire-climax plant does.

The bright golden flowers come most strongly around the time of the spring equinox so the hillsides do indeed seem to burn with gold. The flowers are just in time to feed the newly woken bees – and bees are *sun-beings* and spirit carriers.

In its glowing golden flowers shining in the spring sunshine are flames; the goddess speaks for herself in the watch-phrase – *she* is the blaze on every hill which lights our hearts and hatches the seeds of new growth in us.

Metal: Gold

Onn's metal is gold ... the alchemist's metal.

Gold is a very pure metal and one of three the best conductors of electricity; only silver and copper are more conductive. The word gold comes from an Old English word meaning yellow while its symbol comes from the Latin *aurum*, which means *shining dawn*.

Its beauty has been part of our human history since we first found it and it's the most anciently administered shamanic medicine. It is used in food; gold leaf, flake or dust are used on and in sweets and drinks as decorative ingredient. Danziger Goldwasser (German: Gold water of Danzig) or Goldwasser (English: Goldwater) is a traditional German herbal liqueur produced in what is today Gdańsk, Poland, and Schwabach, Germany, and contains flakes of gold leaf. Taking in gold is to take in the shining dawn.

Planet: Sun

The sun is the star at the centre of the solar system. Physically, it consists of hot plasma interwoven with magnetic fields which act like a dynamo, developing self-amplifying electric currents. These currents are the roots of the solar flares which have enormous effects on our earth, many of which we don't yet understand.

The sun gives us life; without its light and heat there would be no life. Its light enables plants and trees to do photosynthesis – the making of food energy from sunlight and carbon dioxide, and giving us animals its waste-product of oxygen. Without this we wouldn't be able to breathe. Its light energy gives us power although we are still not very good at using it. Its mass keeps the earth in orbit around it, keeping us within its sphere and so able to live.

Concept: Initiation

Initiation is about beginning. It means opening oneself up to new things which can mean burning one's old stuff in order to hatch the seeds of the new. New ideas, training and enabling new skills are all part of this. As we acquire the new skills … and the new perspectives these bring … so we find ourselves entering new worlds. The worlds are new to us because our training has enlarged our vision and we are now able to see them. This new vision gives us access to yet more newness, more new ways of seeing, being and working; it's a form of *permission*, but one we have given to ourselves rather than been granted by some other authority. We give ourselves entry into the worlds.

Onn, Furze, helps us to learn this skill.

F: Fearn: *Alder*

Time: 18 Mar – 14 Apr
Concept: Forgetfulness
Fearn represents our letter F

Alder, *Alnus glutinosa*, is a short-lived species that thrives in damp, cool areas like marshes, wet woodland, and stream and river banks where its roots help to stop soil erosion. It grows well from seed, tolerates poor soil and will quickly colonise bare ground.

Its common name "alder" comes from the Old English *alor*, which in turn comes from Proto-Germanic root *aliso* which derives from the Proto-Indo-European root *el*, meaning red or brown. *El* is also a root for the word elk – which makes me think of our deer goddess, Elen.

Most alders are deciduous. They reproduce by means of elongated male catkins which grow on the same plant as shorter female bud-catkins; both come before leaves appear. They are mainly wind-pollinated, but bees do visit by to a small extent and more so in hard springs when nectar is hard to come by. The female catkins, when mature, look like miniature conifer cones and open in a similar way to release the seeds. The leaves and catkins are food for many butterflies and moths.

Alder has an important symbiotic relationship with *Frankia alni* which is a *nitrogen-fixing* bacterium found in the root nodules. This bacterium absorbs nitrogen from the air and makes it available to the tree; in return, alder provides the bacterium with sugars which it produces through photosynthesis. This mutually beneficial relationship means alder improves the fertility of the soil where it grows and, as a pioneer species (i.e. one that comes first into a barren land) it helps provide additional nitrogen for the plants which follow.

Although a poor firewood alder is often used to smoke food, especially salmon. It gives the best charcoal.

It was used for bridge pillars as the wood does not rot easily in water; indeed most of the pilings that form the foundation of Venice were made from alder trees.

Alder bark contains the anti-inflammatory *salicin*, which is metabolized into salicylic acid in the body. It's been used by shamans to treat problems with insect bites and skin irritations as well as lymphatic disorders and tuberculosis. It's used in smoking mixtures too. Clinical studies have verified that red alder contains *betulin* and *lupeol*, which are effective against a variety of tumours.

As a hardwood, alder is used in making furniture and cabinets, and has been adopted by many electric guitar manufacturers including Fender. In the Pyrenees it's used for making whistle-pipes. The boys of Cerdana, in the Pyrenees, had a charm for the making …

Berng, Berng, come out of your skin
And I will make you whistle sweetly

Berng, or *Verng* in the Majorcan language, is *Bran* and alder is the tree of Bran, one of the elder gods in the British pantheon.

Concept: Forgetfulness

Alder holds the concept of *forgetfulness.*

It's about forgetting the little personal self, your personal wants and needs and focussing instead on the needs of the earth, the goddess. It's about learning to stop being selfish and about learning to serve, learning service … this is Wisdom.

Wisdom means you know that you are just a part of the whole and that, by thinking of the needs of the earth, you can help things work out appropriately. By forgetting your little personal self and focusing on nurturing the earth you actually *enable yourself by enabling others*. So the wheel goes around.

This is true Service.

5th Month – S: Saille: *Willow*

Time: 15 Apr – 12 May
Concept: Boundaries – willow is Brighid's tree
Saille represents our letter **S**

S: Saille: Willow

Willow, Salix, is a water tree. Most species are known as willow, but some narrow-leaved shrub-species are called osier, and some broader-leaved species are referred to as sallow. The word sallow comes from Old English *sealh* which is related to the Latin word *salix*, the ogham name *Saille*, comes from this word.

All willows have lots of watery bark-sap which is heavily charged with *salicylic acid* ... from which comes aspirin. Their wood is soft, pliant and tough and makes wonderful material for making baskets and wattle fences.

It has long, slender branches and large, fibrous, roots which are remarkable for their tenacity to life – the roots will readily regrow when the plant is coppiced which means willow can provide an extremely long-lived source of fuel and building material as our ancestors knew very well. Willow roots will also readily grow from aerial parts of the plant so taking willow cuttings is very easy.

They are very beautiful trees, especially those that have a weeping habit, and they come in a multitude of colours – both stems and leaves – so give a lovely show ranging from yellowish-green through reds to bluish. Often the stems go from silvery-gold through to the reds and purples as well.

Willows produce both male and female flowers as catkins on

different plants. They come early in the spring, often before the leaves or as the new leaves open. The anthers of the flowers are rose-coloured in the bud, but orange or purple after the flower opens; they are very delicate and beautiful.

The leaves and bark of the willow tree have been used as a remedy for aches and fever for millennia. Willow can also relieve headache, stomach-ache, and other body pain.

Willow has been used for making things for thousands of years. Wattle as a technique goes back to Neolithic times; it's a form of lightweight construction material made by weaving thin branches – whole or split – between upright stakes to form a woven lattice. Archaeologists have found fishing net made from willow that dates back over 10,000 years. Baskets, fish traps, wattle fences, wattle and daub house walls, are often woven from willow osiers. One of the forms of Welsh coracle traditionally uses willow in the "lats". Thin or split willow rods can be woven into wicker. Willow wood is also used for boxes, brooms, cricket bats, cradle boards, chairs and other furniture, dolls, flutes, poles, sweat lodges, toys, turnery, tool handles, veneer, wands and whistles. In addition, tannin, fibre, paper, rope and string can all be produced from the wood.

On the ecological front, willows are an excellent source of early pollen for bees. You can eat willow catkins as a mash. Willow is good at bio-filtration – ecological wastewater treatment systems; a willow-water bed construction can even filter heavy metals from water as well as dealing with all the black-water from toilets. They stabilise stream banks and slopes, stop soil erosion, build and reclaim soil, provide shelterbelt, windbreak and wildlife habitat.

Concept: Boundaries

Willow is the tree of boundaries. She is Brighid's tree who, in Welsh, is called Ffraid.

Brighid is a fire goddess as well as being the goddess of

wisdom/poetry, blacksmithing, healing, wells and springs, midwifery and fostering.

As Briga, she is the patron of warfare and her soldiers are called Brigands. Nowadays we are likely to think of brigands as criminals, terrorists or some such but they were warriors and *guardians of boundaries* both in the everyday world and between the worlds. Her warriors guard the boundaries, the thresholds of transition. You'll find more on this in THE CELTIC CHAKRAS.

Boundaries are so important; without them we don't know who, what, where, when or how we are. We need them in order to distinguish between self/not-self; to know what is our shit and what belongs to somebody else that we may have been carrying for them; to know when to act or when to be still and leave well alone. As goddess of healing, Brighid needs us to know all this. Helping, healing, is knowing when to stand back, when to stay out of the way and let something happen rather than trying to save something/one. The feeling to rush in and save someone/thing is just that ... our own emotions driving our own needs and our own wish not to feel the pain of watching someone going through their own shit. The healer has to learn when to allow the person to do their own work and when they really do need help. These are boundaries we all need to learn and willow helps us to do this.

We learn boundaries by knowing opposites, *knowing* the duality of I/Thou. To know light you must know dark. Knowing the pairs of opposites moves us from simplistic concepts of "good" and "bad" to seeing that duality shows us the *two sides of one coin*. Saille, willow, Brighid, teaches us to find, keep and guard our own boundaries, with the aid of her brigands.

Willow & Witches

The word witch may well derive from Proto-Indo European word *weik* which means to separate, to divide ... boundaries again.

In Old English the nouns *wicca* for sorcerer or male witch and *wicce* for sorceress or female witch were used. The Old English verb *wiccian* relates to the Middle Low German and *wichelen* meaning to bewitch. Further etymology of the word is problematic; it has no clear equivalents outside the Old English and Low German. It also give us the word wicker, as in wicker basket or chair ... and in wicker man.

There are sinister folklore stories that the willow is capable of uprooting herself and stalking travellers ... one thinks of triffids!

There is also lore that uses wicker baskets to capture things, including witches. The idea of capturing and controlling witches was used by witch-finders in Cromwellian times and during the witch-hunts in Stuart Britain under King James.

Sheri Tepper picks up this idea in her story of Mavin Manyshaped. Here a shapeshifter could be caught and tamed by being squeezed into a tiny wicker basket so that she or he no longer had "room to shift". There is some validity in the idea however this is a form of dark magic – power over something, controlling – and not one to be followed by the awenydd.

Back in the pre-Christian era witches were loved and revered by their communities; they were the mediums between ordinary folk and otherworld. Christianity found the idea of the wise and cunning folk, and particularly women after the Norman invasion of Britain, too dangerous. Both Normans and church hierarchy considered that awenyddion and cunning folk disabled their ability to control people so Christianity demonised the wise ones and their familiars, spreading falsehoods which are still believed today.

Prior to Christian times otherworld was not strange but a normal part of our everyday world, even if not everyone could see it clearly. Witches, both female and male, were known for wise folk, they were healers; could help people find food and game; could speak with the Ancestors and the Powers; they helped folk transit between life and death, and between otherworld and birth, and the rites of passage throughout life. These knowings, *kennings*, have always been there, hidden amongst the people in "quaint" customs, songs, folk-tales, throughout the past 2,000 years; now they are coming back to light.

6th Month – S/Z: Straif *Blackthorn* & H: Uath *Hawthorn*

Two Goddesses – Ceridwen & Blodeuwedd

This month we have the two thorn trees, the black and the white. They are two faces of the goddess – the Hag in the *blackthorn* and the Maiden in the *whitethorn*.

In the Celtic tradition Ceridwen is the Hag or Crone, the wise old woman who holds the last of winter, while Blodeuwedd is the Flower-Bride who heralds the beginning of summer. Blackthorn flowers before the leaves come at the very end of winter. Whitethorn flowers in May and is also called the May Tree, she holds the beginning of summer.

S/Z: Straif: Blackthorn

Time: 15 Apr – 12 May

Concept: *Retribution* – blackthorn is Ceridwen's tree

Straif represents our letters **S/Z**

Blackthorn

Blackthorn, *Prunus spinosa*, is a member of the rose family, like hawthorn, and native to Europe and western Asia. Its common name, *blackthorn*, comes from its long, dark thorns and its bark which is almost black. The common name for its fruit is "sloes" which comes from Old English *slāh*.

Blackthorn is a small deciduous tree that grows only 7-8m tall, with blackish bark and dense, stiff, spiny branches. Its leaves are oval with a serrated margin. Its flowers, which come shortly before the leaves in early spring, have five creamy-white petals and are pollinated by insects. It is native to Britain and Ireland where it's common in hedges and is often a dominant tree in scrub on heavier soils. Its wood has been used for hundreds (if not thousands) of years for walking sticks and was the traditional wood for Irish shillelaghs.

Blackthorn is a favourite food and nesting plant for many moths. The dead wood in particular provides food for the caterpillars of the concealer moth.

The fruit, the sloes, are like small black plums with a purple-blue waxy bloom, they ripen in autumn and are harvested, in Britain, in October or November after the first frosts; the frost improves the fruit by expanding and breaking the cells. Sloes are thin-fleshed with a very strongly astringent flavour when fresh that really dries the mouth. In Britain and many parts of Europe a lovely alcoholic drink is made by putting the fruit in gin, vodka or brandy along with sugar to produce a liqueur – sloe gin is its best known form. Wine is also made from fermented sloes. The fruit is also used for jam making and in fruit pies. If preserved in vinegar they are similar in taste to Japanese umeboshi plums.

Concept: Retribution

Blackthorn is Ceridwen's tree and, in France, it is called *"La mere du bois"*, the Mother of the Wood. This is a lovely title for Ceridwen who is indeed a Lady of the Wildwood.

Blackthorn is an enchanter's tree. It is the "black rod" that enhances cursings and its thorn will cause deep poisonous wounds; it's the thorn that is used with poppets, dolls that serve as an image upon which a curse is put. This takes us to the idea of retribution.

Retribution is about the righting of wrongs. Arawn, lord of Annwfn which is the name for the Underworld, works with Ceridwen on this; one of his job-titles is "righter of wrongs". He is the lord who partners Ceridwen in this and effects rightings. Both Ceridwen and Arawn are cauldron-keepers of the underworld, the world of the ancestors. They hold the deeds of the past and find ways to balance the consequences of these with deeds from the present and the future. Their cauldrons of rebirth give us new life-jobs in which we can make retribution for past deeds.

Ceridwen gives us back what we give out. This is the settling of scores, paying of debts, retribution, reckoning, justice, payback, settlement, justice. Ponder this. Are there times when such action might be appropriate? Do scores need to be settled? What happens if they're not? Do they stretch on and on into forever, tangling everyone in their sticky web? Blackthorn's ogham name, *Straif*, engendered our word strife – conflict, discord, friction, all of which come about when there is no reckoning for offences.

In current times people can be very "love-n-light", saying they forgive even when there is no contrition for the act. This can be a way of ducking and not dealing with issues, losing one's boundaries and not standing up for principles, none of which is a good thing! Such forgiveness comes only from the head, not from the heart, until there is proper contrition and repayment from the offender. To think you can forgive this way, from the head, is not real, and benefits nobody despite sounding politically correct.

Straif helps us to learn about paying debts, proper exchange, and how to do it successfully. Sometimes it can be very painful but straif helps us learn not to run or hide from conflict, nor to compromise our principles by wanting a peaceful life. Strife is important. People nowadays are often content (especially in the west) with *competition* being a "good thing" but if you call it *strife* then it suddenly becomes unacceptable. We are told "healthy competition" is good but strife is bad. This makes no sense at all.

The concept of retribution is about *exchange*. The word "retribution" comes from the idea of *re-tribute*. To give tribute is to give what is due, to honour a debt and to honour a principle, to pay fairly for what has been given you. It's about payment, fees, tax and duty. When you put "re" in front of a word it signifies a further iteration of the act/thing, it's about doing something over; e.g. re-issue, repeat, re-do. To re-tribute is to give tribute again ... because it has somehow gone astray and not been paid.

Exchange, fair and right exchange, is what the Celtic tradition is about – we *give* and we *take*, both. Taking is also about enabling, it's about *allowing* others to give to you, to tribute you. Giving is about returning that gift of tribute to those who have given to you. This is exchange, a fundamental precept of the Celtic tradition. Exchange may be between human-and-human, human-and-beast, human-and-plant, human-and-the-planet, and it can be between worlds, between the everyday world we live in and otherworld. Wherever we make exchange is a place for retribution, for re-tributing, when things go out of balance.

H: Uath: Hawthorn

Time: 13 May – 9 Jun

Concept: Enabling – hawthorn is Blodeuwedd's tree

Uath represents our letter **H**

Hawthorn's common names include May tree, whitethorn, quickthorn, thornapple, hawberry, hag (Old English), hagthorn, ske (Old Irish) and yorn (pronounced thorn) and porn (Old Norse); it's also known as awes, asogs, boojuns and arzygarzies in various parts of Britain.

Hawthorn is a member of the rose family and native in the temperate regions of the northern hemisphere. This is the region just below the Boreal where Britain now is since the last Ice Age. It's a broadleaf, deciduous tree that can grow up to 12-15m; its bark is brown with shallow scaling ridges and the twigs are slender and brown with long thorns 1-2cm long. The leaves have toothed lobes that are cut at least halfway to the middle mid-rib; their main veins curve outwards and there are tufts of hair on the underside of the leaf where the veins join. Hawthorn tolerates almost every kind of soil but flowers and fruits best in full sun. It's been a common hedging plants in Britain for thousands of years and still is in many places.

The timber is hard and tough and was used for veneer and cabinet work, boxes, tool handles, mill-wheel teeth, mallets and the ribs of small boats. It also makes excellent firewood and charcoal.

May blossom heralds the beginning of summer. Hawthorn is best known perhaps for the traditions of the May Queen who is crowned with May blossom on May Day, the 1st of May. Since Christian times and the dumbing down of the May Queen rituals it's been thought unlucky to bring May flowers into a house.

Hawthorn is an excellent provider of food and shelter for many species of birds, insects and mammals. Their flowers are important for nectar-feeding insects and for the larvae of many butterflies and moths. The fruits, haws, are important wildlife food in winter, particularly for thrushes and waxwings who eat them and disperse the seeds in their droppings.

The bright red haws are good for jams, jellies, juices, ketchups, wines, liqueurs and other drinks all around the northern hemisphere. Some people cook them up with other fruits for a midwinter punch. In several places around the world they are eaten raw as a snack. The leaves are edible and when still young in spring they are tender enough to be used in salads.

Serbian and Croatian folklore says hawthorn is particularly deadly to vampires so stakes to be used for slaying vampires should be made from the wood of the thorn tree.

In Gaelic folklore hawthorn marks the entrance to the other-world and is deeply associated with the Faer. It's very unlucky to cut the tree at any time other than when it is in bloom, usually around Beltane when it is commonly cut for decoration and ritual as the May Bush.

Hawthorn trees are often found beside *clootie* wells and known as *rag trees* because of the invocations written on strips of cloth and tied to the trees as part of wishing/healing rituals.

Susan Cooper uses hawthorn in her novels in THE DARK IS RISING series which are all excellent books and well worth reading for our old lore.

Concept: Enabling

Blodeuwedd is the goddess of this tree. The sweet, heady, sensual scent of the blossom of the may tree is part of her enchantment.

Blodeuwedd's tale is very deep. She is by no means the dippy faithless-wife character that she is usually portrayed in the Victorian stories but a *shapeshifting goddess* and one of the many faces of Sovereignty. Sovereignty is how the Celts think of the Lady, the spirit, the planetary energy, *that which lives and moves and holds our being.* It's a similar concept to how the Dineh people, the Navajo, speak of it; they say Dammas – *that which moves.*

Blodeuwedd's story is of the enabler. She is the woman who teaches the young and heedless boy responsibility ... which is what Gwydion asks of her when he asks her to become his son's wife.

Gwydion, the Master Enchanter of Britain, asks her to help his wastrel son, Llew Llaw Gyffes, become a worthy guardian and king for the Land of Gwynedd. She agrees. In order to do this she asks him to make a form to embody her, for her work in Middleworld for she is a spirit being with no solid shape in the everyday world except her totem, the owl. Gwydion does this by taking nine flowers and making a body to house her spirit. The Hanes Blodeuwedd gives it as follows *(Robert Graves' The White Goddess)...*

Not of father, nor of mother
Was my blood, my body.
I was spellbound by Gwydion,
Prime enchanter of the Britons,
When he formed me from nine blossoms,
Nine buds of various kinds:
From *primrose* of the mountain,
Broom, meadow-sweet and *cockle*,
Together intertwined,
From *bean* in its shade-bearing
A white spectral army
Of earth, and earthly kind,
From blossoms of the *nettle*,
Oak, thorn and bashful *chestnut* –
Nine powers of nine flowers,
Nine powers in me combined,
Nine buds of plant and tree.
Long and white are my fingers
As the ninth wave of the sea.

The flowers Gwydion uses are ...

1 Primrose
2 Broom
3 Meadow-sweet
4 Cockle
5 Bean
6 Nettle
7 Oak
8 Thorn
9 Chestnut

He makes a body for the goddess so that she can work effectively in Middleworld. Once embodied, she initiates Llew into the mysteries of kingship and being guardian to the goddess then, once her job is done, Blodeuwedd returns to her totem form, the owl, the Queen of the Night, and the story ends. You can read my version of the story at www.elensentier.co.uk under Taleweaving.

The Victorian storytellers make Blodeuwedd into a flighty, brainless, faithless female – it seems they were unable to comprehend the underlying story-lore. It is important not to fall into this trap of reducing the goddess to something that fits into your comfort-zone-box. She is a very powerful and enabling face of the goddess and can be formidable.

Her purpose for us – as it was for Llew – is to get us out of our comfort-boxes so that we can awaken and grow. She does this through desire, lust, love, wanting, yearning all of which make us itch and uncomfortable until we move. Blodeuwedd is the initiator and enabler; she harries and teases us through desire and love.

7th Month – U – Ura: *Heather* & D: Duir: *Oak*

U: Ura: *Heather*
Ura, Heather, is the third of the five feasts of the goddess.
Time: Midsummer
Watchwords: *I am the queen of every hive*
Metal: Copper
Planet: Venus
Concept: Consummation
Ura represents our letter **U**

Heather, heath, *ericaceae*, is a family of flowering plants mostly found in acid soils, peat and blanket bogs. It's a huge family with some 4,000 species spread across 126 genera. As well as the heathers we know it includes cranberry, blueberry, huckleberry, azalea, rhododendron, and other common heaths like erica, cassiope, daboecia, and calluna. They're found all over the earth.

It's another fire-plant that needs interaction with fire and regrows readily when it's been burnt. Swaling, the regular controlled burning of the heaths, helps to keep heather young and vigorous. If left unburned it grows long and lank, its nutritional value is reduced, it can get woody and ragged and does not seed well. The heather roots are left undamaged by the swaling and the whole process *shocks* the heather seed, which is lying in the ground, into germinating quickly.

Heather again is food for many animals, insects and birds. Moorland ponies, deer, sheep and cattle also eat it. It's the major breeding ground for golden plover and both merlin and hen harrier breed there as well as curlew, short-eared owl, meadow pipit, whinchat dunlin, skylark and nightjar. Birds who feed on the animals who live on heather moorland include golden eagle, peregrine, raven, dotterel, osprey and goshawk. Both bumblebees and honeybees love it, butterflies, moths and flies all feed on heather and they attract birds who feed on them. As you can see, it's very important habitat.

Heather wood can be used for carving. It's another of the Bach flower remedies. Heather helps people who lack empathy or concern for others and are only concerned with themselves and their own problems; folk who get like this will often *invade your space*.

Time: Midsummer

Midsummer solstice is the other side of the coin to midwinter. From midsummer to midwinter there is gradually less and less light each day. It's one the four sun-feasts which must have been important to us as long as there have been humans on the planet to notice them. At Stonehenge and other circles around Britain, stones mark the midsummer sunrise.

Like all traditions that follow lunar calendars, midsummer celebrations begin at dusk on the eve of the day, at the moment when the sun sets. Bonfires are built, cattle driven between them, people jump over them, wicker statues are burnt in them – all are celebrations of the sun. Other old customs include collecting bones and burning them, making smoke to carry wishes and invocations across to the otherworld; making firebrands and carrying them round the fields, fire wheels and barrels are still made and rolled down the hill. The fires and wheels celebrate the sun; they are an invocation, invitation, to the star which gives us life ... the sun.

Watchwords

The watchwords for ura, heather, are, *"I am the queen of every hive"*.

This brings us to the bee again. In many traditions the bee is one of the creatures that carries our spirit between the worlds.

Midsummer is the time when bees swarm, when the queen leaves the hive and the bees follow her. She flies high, dances and calls to the male bees. Those who are able to keep up with her, catch her, get to mate with her and so a new brood, a new hive, is formed.

The goddess is queen of the hive. Like the queen bee she tests potential mates, candidates for kingship, in order to choose her king as the queen bee tests the male bees in her flight, to see who is up for the job.

In nature it is usually the male who has to impress the females, to show them that his genes are the best, that he is the one who should father the young. Sometimes this happens in finding just one mate as with swans and ravens for instance. For herd animals, like the stag or hart, the male seeks to impress all the females by shouting and fighting; if he succeeds it will be his genes that go forward in the herd. Then there are the complex relations of the wolf-pack which is truly ruled by the Lady and Lord. The alpha male and female are supported by the rest of the pack, but it is only the alpha female who will breed. They keep the pack to a size which can support itself.

In all cases it is *she* who is the goddess' representative ... *she* who chooses. This is what ura teaches us ... the feminine in all of us, whatever our gender, is the spirit that chooses and rules. Once this is understood the masculine takes on its wonderful role of guardian of the goddess and stops either competing or trying to control. This is true whether it's our relationship with ourselves or our relationships with others.

Metal: Copper

Pure copper is soft and malleable metal with very high thermal and electrical conductivity. It is a beautiful reddish-orange colour and is known to have been used for at least 10,000 years. When combined with tin (Jupiter's metal) it makes bronze. There is evidence that gold and meteoric iron (but not iron smelting) were the only metals used by humans before copper.

Planet: Venus

The seven heavenly bodies known to the ancients were each associated with the seven metals known in antiquity and Venus was assigned to copper. Venus is the second planet from the sun. She is one of the brightest objects in the sky and has been known since prehistoric times.

Concept: Consummation

The queen of every hive is the Lady of Choices ... she requires to be given choice in order to be her true self; and this goes for all beings, plants, planets, animals and people.

Consummation is the first act of sexual intercourse between two people following their wedding to each other. It is a moment of deep spiritual significance and commitment; you have committed to a choice and you allow each other choice for consummation is not rape.

The story of Ragnall's Wedding, tells this beautifully and is the story associated with Duir, oak, who partners Ura. You can read this story at www.elensentier.co.uk ; it is one of the most significant stories in the British tradition as it affirms the importance of choice. As Ragnall says, *"And in this choice lies Sovereignty"*.

What do all people, indeed all creatures, want? The ability to choose. And how often do we take this from them?

The queen of every hive is Sovereignty, one of the titles we give the goddess in the Celtic tradition. She teaches us to be

sovereign to ourselves and so able to allow sovereignty in others
… this is the potential of choice.

D: Duir; Oak

Time: 10 Jun – 7 Jul
Concept: Oak is the tree of the D*oor*
Duir represents our letter **D**

English oak (Quercus robur) is the most common tree in Britain.
Mature oaks reach around 20m in height and their leaves are
distinctive with deep lobes and smooth edges. The fruit, acorns,
are not produced until the tree is at least 40 years old and peaks
between 80-120 years. They have long stalks and are held in the
cups known as fairy-cups. They are a rich food source for wildlife
and humans; you can make both a form of coffee and flour from
them. Traditionally the leaves, bark and acorns were believed to
heal many medical ailments including diarrhoea, inflammation
and kidney stones. Tannin, found in the bark, is used for tanning
leather.

Oaks form a broad, spreading crown with an open canopy
that allows enables light to reach through to the woodland floor
for bluebells and primroses. The smooth and silvery brown bark
becomes rugged and deeply fissured as they age. Oak tree
growth is rapid in youth but gradually slows at around 120 years;
they even get shorter as they grow older in order to extend their
lifespan.

Oak forests provide a habitat rich in biodiversity and support
more life forms than any other of our native trees, hosting over
280 species of insect and supplying many birds with an
important food source. In autumn many woodland birds and

mammals including jays, mice and squirrels, badgers and deer eat the acorns and they once were a major source of autumn food for pigs when they were kept in the woods, as some still are in Britain. Oak leaves break down easily in autumn to form a rich leaf mould under the tree which supports invertebrates like stag beetles as well as numerous fungi like the oakbug milkcap. Pied flycatchers and marsh tits use holes and crevices in the tree-bark as nesting spots. Several British bat species roost in old woodpecker holes or under loose bark and feed on the rich supply of insects in the tree canopy.

Oaks produce one of the hardest and most durable timbers on the planet, prized for thousands of years, even its Latin name, *Quercus robur*, means strength. It takes at least 150 years before an oak is ready to use for building so foresting oaks covers several generations. It was the primary ship building material until the mid-19th century and is still a popular wood for architectural beams.

World Tree

Oak is the World Tree for Britain. It is the doorway between worlds and so the World Tree of the British tradition. Its name,

Duir, comes from the Sanskrit *Dwr* meaning door. Midsummer is its flowering season and oak galls are known as Serpent Eggs. They are thunder and lightning trees, prone to lightning strikes being often the tallest living thing in the landscape.

This picture comes from an ancient grove in Derby and shows an oak tree with its branches and roots entwined in the circle of life.

Archaeological evidence of our use of oak as central to our world-view goes back at least 4,500 years as we found with the discovery of Seahenge in 1998.

Seahenge was discovered by an amateur archaeologist John Lorimer in 1998 at Holme-next-the-Sea, near Old Hunstanton in Norfolk. It is a timber circle with an upturned tree root in the centre and was built during the early Bronze Age, some 4,500 years ago.

Time Team built a replica of it that was most impressive and gave you a strong sense of what the place must have been about. Time Team is a British Channel 4 archaeology series which has a team of specialists carrying out an archaeological dig over a three day period, with actor Tony Robinson explaining what they find

in layman's terms.

The idea of burying the tree upside-down conveys the concept of the 3 Worlds. Upperworld is fed by the wisdom of Lowerworld and vice versa. Middleworld, the trunk of the tree, is the pathway and door between worlds.

The roots hold the ancestral wisdom, Lowerworld in the British tradition. Tree roots draw nourishment, water and food from the earth/soil with the aid of mycorrhiza. Mycorrhizas form a *mutualistic* beneficial relationship with the roots of plants. This relationship provides the fungus with constant direct access to carbohydrates and, in return, the mycelium improves the plant's ability to absorb water and minerals. Mycorrhiza are like a physical counterpart of the web of life.

The branches symbolise the Upperworld in the British tradition. They hold all the potential, the latent budding, conceivable and embryonic concepts of life which have yet to become manifest.

Their leaves perform that most amazing feat of energy-change … photosynthesis. Photosynthesis is when plants convert light energy into chemical energy which is fuel/food for them ... and for us. Plants make carbohydrates from carbon dioxide and water using the energy of sunlight. At the same time they release oxygen as a "waste product" from their own food-making which means we have an atmosphere we can breathe. Indeed, photosynthesis supplies most of the energy necessary for all life on earth!!!

The trunk symbolise the Middleworld in the British tradition and connects the roots and the branches, the Lower and Upper worlds. All the pathways and connections between them flow through the trunk.

Understanding the trunk of a tree is key to understanding how a tree works. The trunk connects the crown with its roots. Roots absorb water and nutrients from the soil; these are then transported up the tree trunk in cells that act like pipes, feeding the leaves and flowers and so making the fruits. The trunk is how the leaves obtain water and nutrients to do the magic of photosynthesis. Then the food made in the leaves is transported down to the roots to enable the tree to grow.

So ... the trunk of the World Tree – Middleworld – does this for the Upper and Lower worlds. And we, as part of Middleworld, are here to do our part in this.

Concept: Oak King – Guardianship

Duir, oak, flowers at midsummer and is the companion of ura, heather. Together they expand our *kenning* of the relationship between the goddess, the queen of every hive, and the god, the Oak King.

Sir James Frazer's study of European mythologies, THE GOLDEN BOUGH, describes how the Oak King is killed at midsummer by the Holly King. At midwinter, the Oak King returns and the roles are reversed. The two kings are guardians of Sovereignty and each guards her for one half of the year; the Oak King from midwinter to midsummer and the Holly King from midsummer to midwinter.

The Oak King is the lord of the sky and the fire at the heart of the sun while the Holly King is the lord of darkness and the underworld, the fire at the heart of the earth. Between the two of them they hold Middleworld. Middleworld is the maiden-spirit that the stories tell of who is fought over by winter and summer. This is the endless cycle of death and rebirth as shown in the oak tree disc where the branches and roots are intertwined.

8th Month – T: Tinne: *Holly*

Time: 8 Jul – 4 Aug
Concept: Sacrifice
Tinne represents our letter **T**

T: Holly

Holly, *Ilex aquifolium*, is in the family of Aquifoliaceae, found worldwide from the tropics to temperate zones and from sea level to more than 2,000 metres for the high mountain species. It is a small, evergreen tree, often slow-growing but, given time, some can grow to 25m tall.

Holly plants have simple, alternate, glossy leaves, with a spiny-toothed serrated leaf margin. Their flowers are small and delicate, greenish white with four petals. They come on different plants so you need a tree of each gender for the female to fruit. The flowers are sometimes eaten by moth larva.

The fruit ripens in autumn into the wonderful red berries of the midwinter season ... if the birds don't eat them all! Holly berries are vital winter food for many species of birds and other wild animals. In the autumn and early winter the fruits are hard and apparently unpalatable but after being frozen or frosted several times they soften and become milder in taste. They are toxic to humans but their poisonous properties are much overstated and fatalities are practically unknown. During winter storms birds often take refuge in hollies as they provide evergreen shelter, protection from predators and food all in one.

Ilex in Latin means holm-oak or evergreen oak (*Quercus ilex*). Despite the Linnaean classification of ilex as holly, as late as the

19th century in Britain, the term ilex was still being applied to oak as well as holly.

The origin of the word "holly" is thought to be a reduced form of Old English *hole(ġ)n*, Middle English *Holin*, later *Hollen*. The French word for holly is *houx* and derives from the Old Low Franconian *hulis* (Middle Dutch *huls*). Both are related to Old High German *hulis, huls*, as do Low German/Low Franconian terms like *Hülse* or *hulst*. These Germanic words appear to be related to words for holly in Celtic languages, such as Welsh *celyn*, Breton *kelen(n)* and Irish *cuileann*.

Holly was often used in the construction of weapons, and is known as a plant of warriors and protectors. It's been used as a protection plant for millennia and is often hung above entrances, doors, windows. A holly hedge is good physical protection as well – its spiky leaves will keep most people and animals out as well as providing winter shelter and protection to birds and small animals.

In the past, boiled young holly leaves were used as a cure for colds, bronchitis and rheumatism and, because they are poisonous, the berries were recommended as a laxative!

We use the red holly berries along with the black berries of ivy and the white berries of mistletoe to celebrate midwinter and sun-return. Bringing in evergreen branches to decorate homes and barns at midwinter is a custom which goes back far beyond Christian times. The early Christian church carefully selected pagan celebration dates as a time to introduce Christian themes so holly became a Christmas symbol. Christians took holly as a charm against witches, goblins and the devil – i.e. awenyddion and other cunning folk.

Concept: Sacrifice

Traditionally the Holly King (the summer king) is killed by the Oak King (the winter king) at the winter solstice. The tale is told in the story of GAWAIN AND THE GREEN KNIGHT where Gawain, as tánaiste, accepts the challenge for Arthur. The story is a beheading-game.

The Holly King, Green Man or Green Knight, comes to disturb Arthur's midwinter feast with his beheading game. He is Arthur's conscience, the lurker at the threshold who will not allow the king to become moribund. The story goes …

The Green Knight rides into Arthur's hall bearing a huge bunch or bush of his totem holly and an enormous double-headed axe. He is completely green, his skin, hair, his horse, clothes and all the trappings of the horse. He asks who will play his game, offering to allow his challenger to cut off his head provided that, a year and a day later, he may be offered the chance to cut off the head of his opponent. This sounds easy – how can a headless man be a threat? But, of course, it isn't easy and the Green Man is one of the powers of the earth.

Gawain, as Arthur's tánaiste, accepts the challenge. The Green Man gives Gawain the axe and kneels down, baring his neck for the stroke. Gawain wields the axe and cuts off his head … then the magic happens. The Green Man gets up, walks over to where his head has rolled, picks it up and tucks it under his arm. He then mounts his horse and turns to Gawain saying he'll see him in a year, then he rides off back into the enchanted forest! Gawain takes up the challenge and succeeds in working out what he must do. If you'd like to read the whole story go to www.elen.sentier.co.uk and look under "Stories".

The severed head is one of the fundamental tenets of the British and Celtic traditions. We know the head as "the seat of wisdom and of the soul"; Caitlin Mathews explains some of this in her book ENCYCLOPEDIA OF CELTIC WISDOM. We did not worship severed heads, per say, but knew the head as the Cave of Bright Darkness where the light of spirit is seated.

John Barelycorn

Gawain and the Green Knight's story and the time of tinne link us to John Barleycorn. This is another prepared and agreed sacrifice of the king to the land. Nowadays it's perhaps better known through Frazer, in THE GOLDEN BOUGH, where he tells us of the Greek Eleusinian ritual, in which Kerkyon the "year-King"(Kerkyon is a title, not a name), is required to do battle and give his life at the harvest time for the good of his kingdom. He would be succeeded by the victor just as he himself had succeeded the previous king a year earlier.

The old British song of John Barelycorn shows us how the goodness, the seed, of the king (John Barleycorn) is put back into the earth to grow and harvest for us year on year. It is the story of the grain-harvest and the cycle of death and rebirth that mirrors the rhythms of the earth. Look it up on Google.

9th Month – C: Coll: *Hazel* & Q: Quert: *Apple*

Again this month we have the two trees sharing the time. As with the two thorn trees, hazel and apple are two faces of the goddess, in this case the faces of *wisdom* and *kenning*.

C: Coll: Hazel
Time: 5 Aug – 1 Sep
Concept: Hazel is the tree of *wisdom*
Coll represents our letter C

The hazel tree (*Corylus avellana*) is member of the birch family (*Betulaceae*). The fruit, hazel nuts, are variously called filbert, hazelnut or cobnut depending on the relative length of the nut to its husk. Hazel is common throughout Britain and Europe. More of a large shrub than a tree, its average height is 3½-6 meters though it has been recorded growing up to 18 meters. It likes to grow in copses as well as in oak woods and hedgerows, and thrives in damp places near ponds and streams, however it fruits better in well-drained land.

Hazel has been grown and coppiced for millennia. Its wood is a whitish-red and has a close, even grain, its smooth, straight stems are tough and elastic and used for hampers, hoops, wattles and baskets. Beautiful, well-veined veneers are made from its larger roots. It is also used for walking sticks, shepherds' crooks, fishing rods and rustic seats. It makes good artists' charcoal and the charcoal is good for gunpowder too, although willow charcoal is said to be better for explosives.

Hazel is also used widely for spirit-protection. Scotland's old name, Caledonia, derives from Caldun meaning *fort of the hazel*. The word *cnocach* means wisdom and comes from a common word for hazelnut, *cno*. In Gaelic lore Finn bore a hazelwood shield that made him invincible in battle. No harm could penetrate a hurdle fence of hazel around a house or a breastband of hazel wood on a horse. A shipmaster wearing a cap into which hazel had been woven was guaranteed to weather any storm. Cattle driven through Beltaine and midsummer bonfires had their backs singed with hazel rods for protection against disease and the evil eye, and the scorched rods were used to drive them the rest of the year. In the east of England, cottagers gathered hazels to use homoeopathically against the bolts of the thunder-god. In Ireland, a hazel-nut in the pocket warded off rheumatism and lumbago which were thought to be caused by *elfshot*; and a double-nut prevented toothache. An old charm for curing an adder bite was to place a piece of hazel wood in the shape of an equal-armed cross on the wound.

In the north of England, the hazel-tree guardian was called "Melsh Dick" and in Yorkshire "Chum-milk Peg" – a milk peg is a milk tooth, the tooth of childhood. In 19th century Devon, an old woman traditionally greeted a new bride with a gift of hazels for fertility.

The world is sometimes likened to a hazel nut and a forked hazel twig is used for dowsing.

Concept: Fire in the Head – Wisdom

I went out to the hazelwood,
Because a fire was in my head,
W. B. Yeats

Yeats was a man of the Faer. The *fire in the head* he speaks of is wisdom; it sets light to your current habits and patterns and reduces them to ashes … it forces you to get out of the box!

Hazel, wisdom and salmon are all intricately connected in the Celtic tradition. The Salmon of Wisdom travels his long journey round the world each year from and to the Well at World's End (the Well of Segais) which is surrounded by 9 hazel trees. He goes to catch the falling hazelnuts of wisdom before returning to "the ways of the round rolling world". In Gaelic stories Finn is cooking a salmon when (like in the story of Taliesin) some boiling juice falls on his thumb, Finn licks his burnt thumb and swallows a drop of the magic juice so gaining the gift of prophecy.

In the Greek tradition, Hermes' staff – the caduceus – is made of a hazel wand up which twine two snakes. It is still the symbol of healing today. The original rod had hazel leaves instead of the wings we see nowadays.

I said at the beginning of this chapter that hazel tree is member of the birch family and this gives us another connection to Elen. Coll, hazel, is Elen's tree and in the roots of birch trees is a favourite place for the fly agaric mushroom to grow. Fly agaric is the mushroom the reindeer eat, the shamans then collect their pee and drink it. Passing through the reindeer's body causes the mushroom to lose the toxins that humans cannot take. This leaves it with its journeying properties so the shaman can give it to the people to enable them to walk between worlds for a few hours without having to go through the shaman training.

Q: Qwert: Apple

Time: 5 Aug – 1 Sep

Concept: Apple is the tree of *knowing* and *reincarnation*

Quert represents our letter Q

Apple

Crab apple (Malus sylvestris) is the most important ancestor of the cultivated apple (of which there are more than 6,000 varieties), it grows throughout Europe, thrives in heavy soil in hedgerows, woods and areas of scrub and can live to up to 100 years.

It's been found in British bronze-age sites and has been grown for thousands of years in Europe and Asia. Apples are present in the mythology of many cultures including Celtic, Norse and Greek traditions.

Mature trees grow to around 10m in height. They have an irregular, rounded shape and a wide, spreading canopy. Their bark can become quite gnarled and twisted, especially when exposed, and the twigs often develop spines and this "crabbed" appearance may have influenced the tree's common name, "crab apple".

Unlike many trees, the crab apple usually grows alone and sometimes woods will only have one tree. The brown, pointed leaf buds form on short stalks and have downy hair on their tips and are followed by glossy, oval leaves. In spring, the sweetly scented blossom is pollinated by bees and other insects. The flowers develop into small, yellow-green apple-like fruits;

sometimes the fruits are flushed with red or white spots when ripe. Birds and mammals eat the fruit and disperse the seeds.

The leaves are food for the caterpillars of many moths; the flowers provide a source of early pollen and nectar for insects, particularly bees, and the fruit is eaten by birds, including blackbirds, thrushes and crows as well as mammals like mice, voles, foxes and badgers.

The long flowering period of crab apples makes them excellent pollination partners for cultivated apples. The fruit can be roasted and served with meat, added to ales or punches, and made into crab apple jelly. It's also a good natural source of pectin, for setting jams.

Its pinkish wood makes good quality timber and is very good for carving and turning. It makes a sweet-scented firewood too. A yellow dye can be made from the bark.

The Proto-Celtic word *aballo*, apple, is the root from which the name of Avalon derives; Brythonic old Welsh, Cornish and Breton share these roots. In old Welsh *abal* is apple and *aball* is apple tree; in Middle Welsh it's spelt *aval, avall* and in Modern Welsh it's *afal, afall*. In Breton, apple is spelled *aval, avaloù* in plural.

In the British tradition one the most famous connections with the apple is Merlin in his "mad" phase in the Caledonian Forest (remember Caledonia's name comes from Col, hazel, which pairs with apple) with his companion pig. Merlin, deep in the forest, eats the apples of knowing.

The word *avalon* means apple and apple is the reincarnation fruit of the Isle of Avalon. It's also the otherworld island home of Manawyddan – Manannán mac Lir and Emain Ablach in Old Irish. The island's other names include West-over-the-Sea. The Elysian fields of the Greek tradition are the "apple lands" too and Apollo's name, the Greek sun god, means apple-man. Cut in half, crosswise as opposed to from stem to base, the five seeds make the five-pointed star, pentacle-pattern, of many initiation-cults.

The connections between the Brythonic and the Irish Gaelic

stories of – are about the "apple lands"; Ablach means "having apple trees" from the Old Irish *aball*, apple.

Apples are the life-giving fruit of Avalon, the Isle of Rebirth for the British tradition. Many of the islands around the west coast of Britain are said to be Avalon; Lundy Island, just off the coast of Bideford near where I grew up is one of them. They are the Isles of the Dead, West-Over-the-Sea and many other names in our tradition, all of which are associated with the Faer, with otherworld and the land from which we come at birth into this world and to which we return at death.

Apples are the fruit of wisdom and of life. If you cut an apple crosswise you see the 5 pips laid out like a 5-pointed star (associated with Venus). They are also the fruit of the Elysian Fields, that name too means apple-land.

Avalon is the *isle of apples*. Apples are magical in so many traditions around the world, wherever they will grow. Avalon or Ynys Afallon is renowned through British history and mythology. In written historical records it first appears in Geoffrey of Monmouth's HISTORIA REGUM BRITANNIAE (The History of the Kings of Britain) as the place where King Arthur's sword Excalibur (Caliburn) was forged and later where Arthur was taken after the Battle of Camlan.

Crab apple is one of the few host trees for mistletoe, *Viscum album*, another magical plant but not one of the ogham trees.

Concept: Kenning

The word kenning means to know. This is not about having knowledge of something, not to have learned about something, but to know it deeply in your bones.

Apples are the fruits of truth in many traditions where the trees grow. When you eat the apple you know things, things you may never have suspected before.

This kind of knowing, kenning, is what the awenydd, the shaman, has. The Tungus word shaman means one who knows.

This kind of knowing may have no logic or mental-thinking attached to it but once you have it you are certain beyond any kind of rationalisation that may be put to you.

As an example, try this idea. If I throw a bucket of water over you then you know, absolutely, that you're wet! You don't need a weekend course, or to read it in a book, or be told it by some expert with alphabet soup after their name. You know, without any doubt or rationalisation, that you're wet!

Kenning, knowing, for the awenydd is like this.

10th Month – E – Eadha: *Poplar* & M: Muin: *Bramble*

E: Eadha: Poplar

Eadha, poplar, is the fourth of the five feasts of the goddess.

Time: Autumn equinox

Watchwords: *I am the shield to every head*

Metal: Iron

Planet: Mars

Concept: Repose

Eadha represents our letter **E**

Poplar Trees

Poplar, *Populus tremula* and its far rarer cousin *Populus nigra* (black poplar), is the shield-maker's tree, the tree of the elders, the wize-ards and cunning folk.

Other old names for poplar are *Aespe* (Anglo-Saxon), *Eadha* (Old Irish), *Crithionn* (Gaelic), *Aps* (southern England), *Pipple* (south-west England), *Quakin' ash* (Scotland).

They are beautiful, delicate trees with whispering leaves that shiver and shudder at the slightest breeze, telling the secrets of the earth. In the westering sun the trees appear to twinkle. Its Latin name *tremula* means to tremble from the way the leaves flutter and move with the least breath of air.

Black poplar is a declining species and rarely found; it grows in isolation in boggy ground such as in wet woodland or on flood plains. We are fortunate here – we live in marshland – as there are two black poplars right by my bedroom window; they're over seventy years old now and tawny owls often sing from them at midnight.

The male and female flowers, catkins, of the black poplar form on separate trees meaning you need one of each to produce seed. The male catkins are red while the female catkins are yellow-green; they're wind pollinated and, when fertilised, the female catkins develop into fluffy cotton-like seeds, which fall in late summer.

White poplar is the whitest tree in the landscape, and from a distance it can appear to be covered in snow due to the woolly white hairs on the leaves and shoots.

Its leaves are heart-shaped, long-tipped and small with a mild balsam scent. The purple catkins flower in mid-spring, later the white, fluffy fruits litter the ground in mid-May. Its dark brown bark often appears black because of the deep craggy fissures and burrs while its twigs are knobbly and amber in colour. It likes damp places; as where we live used to be marsh the trees are very happy here.

Poplar creeps through land, spreading by suckers from the root system so one tree will create an entire grove. Individual trees can live for 40–150 years but the colony-root-system can live for thousands of years, sending up new trunks as the older trunks die off above ground. One such colony in Utah is said to be 80,000 years old and probably the oldest living colony in the world. Because of their longevity poplars are an indicator of ancient woodlands. They can survive forest fires because the roots are below the burning heat; new sprouts grow out of the ashes. Young trees need sun as seedlings can't grow when shaded by mature trees; fire opens up the area to sunlight.

Poplar wood is light but tough, absorbs shock and resists splintering. It's ancient use was for wooden shields, the bottom of carts, floors of oast houses (as it is resistant to fire), matches and for baskets. The bark is an important host for bryophytes which are food plants for the larvae of several butterfly species. Young bark is important seasonal forage for the European hare and other animals in early spring; it's also a tree of choice for the European beaver.

Time: Autumn Equinox

The equinoxes are times of stillness, like the centre of a spinning wheel, which is actually still, or like the eye of the storm. At the outer edges of this spinning wheel of the year are the solstices, winter and summer, dark and light, birth and death. It is these that hold the poles, the extremes. Between them they create the point of tension, the still point of the equinoxes.

Autumn hold the other side of the coin to spring. The earth hovers over the equinox before she turns down into the darkness of winter. The time from autumn to spring is a one of deep work within the soil and the roots of plants which enables them to rise up again in the spring, to grow and flower and fruit for the autumn harvest.

We need darkness as much as light. The two work together to make the whole – day/night, waking/sleep, the pairs of opposites that make up the whole, the one. Poplar teaches us this.

Watchwords

The watchwords for Eadha, poplar, are *I am the shield to every head.*

A poplar shield would be strong, light, tough and fire-resistant. It sounds very useful … so how do we work spiritually with this?

The idea of a shield is more than just a piece of wood carried in battle. Many of us feel we do need one in everyday life which can be a battle in itself. Poplar can teach us about invisible, force-field-like shields we can create around us, built to fit and to guard us in the most appropriate way.

The watchwords particularly speak of the *head* – the shield for every head. What is this about? If you go back to Col, hazel, you'll remind yourself of WB Yeats' words …

I went out to the hazelwood,
Because a fire was in my head,

The *fire in the head* he speaks of is wisdom, remember. We need to guard this wisdom, from everything. It is our ability to *ken*, to *know*, not a mere collection of knowledge although it needs knowledge to fuel the fire of kenning. The light in the head is very special; we all have it but it doesn't *come to light* until we are conscious of it.

Once we do, once it's alight within our head, we need to shield it from others, and to shield them from this light; it's fierce and can damage those who are not aware of it. Poplar teaches us how to do this.

The poplar shield is strong: it can resist both our inner desire to fire up and the desire of others to attack this strange sense within us which frightens them.

The poplar shield is light: it is light in the sense of allowing light in, and out; and it's light in the sense of not being heavy and in the way.

The poplar shield is tough: it's tough enough not to allow others in and to protect you.

The poplar shield is fire-resistant: fire in the head certainly needs that!

Metal: Iron

Iron is the most common element on planet earth, the fourth most common element in the earth's crust; it forms much of earth's outer and inner core. It's been mined since ancient times and gave its name to the Iron Age; but iron from meteorites has been used even longer, for more than 7,000 years.

Iron is vital for our blood, and for the respiration and oxidation processes in plants and animals. It forms complexes with molecular oxygen in the haemoglobin in the blood; it is an oxygen-transport protein in all vertebrates; without it we wouldn't live.

Planet: Mars

Mars is the most earth-like of the planets in our solar system. It has a thin atmosphere and surface features which remind us of the craters on the moon. It also has volcanoes, including the second highest mountain in the solar system, about 16.7 miles high. Mount Everest is just under 5.5 miles high! It also valleys, deserts, and polar ice caps like earth and seems to have similar seasons. It's red because it has a very high iron content.

Concept: Repose

The concept for Eadha is *repose*. Poplar's shield-role helps us learn this.

Repose is about *being still*; it's about being cool, calm and composed, level-headed. Its opposite is worry, tension and stress – things many people feel in their everyday lives. If you stop panicking and stay still for a moment your body and mind *relax* from the adrenalin rush the situation has brought on; your head gets clearer and so your mind is protected. You can see your position better and there's enough space-time for helpful ideas to come in.

Being still is one of the fundamental skills of the shaman … you stand at the still-point, in the eye of the storm, the still-point of the equinox and so become better able to face going forward again.

M: Muin: Bramble

Time: 2 Sep – 29 Sep
Concept: *Thread-twining*
Muin represents our letter M

Brambles are thorny plants of the genus Rubus. The name, bramble, refers to the fruit of any plant in this genus which includes both blackberry and raspberry. The word originates from the German *bram-bezi,* along with *brombeere* and the French word *framboise.*

It's a vine-like plant and very fast growing with hard woody stems that is found in hedgerows, scrub, heathland, woodlands and any ground left uncultivated. It thrives in most soils, in sun, partial or even full shade.

Bramble bushes have grown by sending long, arching canes upwards from a perennial rootstock each spring. The canes have a two-year "life span" producing leaves on their first year shoots and flowers on the lateral shoots in the second year. All brambles bear edible fruit; the fruits are aggregate, with many small units – drupelets – to each fruit. The green berries appear in July, gradually darkening to black by August. Eaten raw, cooked in pies, jams and in a variety of ways, bramble has formed part of the human diet in Western Europe for thousands of years. Examination of "Haraldskaer woman" indicated that blackberries formed part of her diet.

Bramble is good for wildlife. The flowers attract numerous nectar-feeding insects, bees, butterflies and hoverflies, and are an important food plants for their larvae. Birds, especially blackbirds, and various mammals feed on the autumn fruits.

Bramble is sometimes planted in British native mixed hedges to help *bind the whole together* and make a stronger barrier. Robins, wrens, thrushes, blackbirds, warblers and finches all nest in bramble-hedge and small mammals use it for protection from predators. Many moths (including buff arches, peach blossom and fox) lay their eggs on bramble for their larvae to feed on. The hooked thorns, as well as deterring grazing animals from eating them, also help to support the plant by latching onto other vegetation as it grows.

Split bramble stems are traditionally used as binding material for straw in production of basketry, chairs and bee skeps.

The stems can easily grow to five metres and, when they run out of support, the tip of the stem droops to the ground, takes root, and sends up a new plant. In this way the blackberry can leap-frog across country and colonise new fields. Large amounts of bramble covering an area will change the microclimate beneath it; while it can offer protection to young tree seedlings from grazing and browsing animals, it can also suppress the development of light loving species.

Blackberry wine is good and has been part of the tradition of the countryside for millennia. Cunning folk make a potent brew to aid in walking between the worlds. They also make excellent fruit pies, jams and cordials. Brambles can be an astringent or a tonic, the leaves and roots are used in holistic remedies; such as to aid with diarrhoea. Chewing the leaves is said to be a 2,000-year-old remedy for bleeding gums.

From just after the autumn equinox blackberries are left for the animals, faer folk and birds. Brambles sometimes surround the faery rings as a barrier to those who have not asked to come in – asking is vital to walking between the worlds.

Concept: Thread-Twining

Bramble is about thread-twining ... the ability to weave your own consciousness thread with that of another *willing* being. It's about how you twine your consciousness with the consciousness of everything else ... connecting with everything.

When you twine your consciousness thread with that of another, be it animal, plant, person, otherworldly being, you *share* their consciousness, their knowing, seeing, hearing, smelling, tasting and touching – and they share yours. It's perhaps the most intimate contact anyone can have with another and it's akin to shapeshifting.

To experience it changes your whole way of thinking with regard to otherness. It's what Taliesin means when he speaks his long "I have been ..." soliloquy. When you *have been* something in the sense of thread-twining you can never again consider cruelty towards it, your way of life and living is changed.

Bramble's manner of leapfrogging across the countryside and connecting it all together shows us something of this. It can root anywhere, just by touching its stem-tip to the ground, and so create new plants.

This ability to twine threads is essential to the awenydd; the work cannot be done unless you are willing to do this ... *and* to allow both otherworld and the spirits that live with you in the thisworld to twine with you.

As modern humans we are taught, perhaps even from birth from our parents' attitudes, to believe we should be "in charge", "in control", able to "fix things", able to "handle" things, you probably recognise what I'm saying. And all these attitudes have only caused us to make a complete mess of the earth as well as disconnecting us from her. We no longer ask; we no longer listen. We make assumptions, know best, "know what you mean"; we *translate* what someone says into what we think they mean! The gods preserve us ... well perhaps they shouldn't!

If you have the self-confidence to ask a rose, your cat, the fridge even, let alone another human being, "how may I help you?" and you then have the nous and gumption to listen without making assumptions and translations, then you will learn so very much. This ability to ask and listen is fundamental to achieving thread-twining.

If you do not listen, if you make assumptions, if you translate, then you are attempting to control! Bramble, if you allow it, will help you lose this ridiculous and cruel trait you've likely learned since birth. It's well worth it.

11th Month – G: Gort: *Ivy*

Time: 30 Sep – 27 Oct
Concept: Ivy is the tree of *Exchange*
Gort represents our letter **G**

G: Gort: Ivy

Ivy, *Hedera helix*, is native to most of Europe and western Asia. It's a rampant, clinging evergreen vine and a familiar sight in gardens, waste spaces, on house walls, tree trunks and in wild areas across the country. Hedera is the generic name for ivy; *helix* comes from Ancient Greek meaning to twist, turn … spiral.

Ivy climbs by means of aerial rootlets with matted pads which cling strongly to surfaces like rock, walls, trees and cliffs. It also covers the ground if no vertical surfaces are available.

Ivy leaves are alternate and may be either the palmate, five-lobed juvenile leaves which grow on the creeping and climbing stems, or the unlobed, cordate adult leaves that grow on the fertile flowering stems which are high in the crowns of trees or the top of rock faces and exposed to full sun. It produces its flowers from late summer to late autumn. They are small, umbels of greenish-yellow and very rich in nectar and an important late autumn food for bees and other insects. The fruits are purple-black berries that ripen in late winter and are important food for birds. The berries are somewhat poisonous to humans. Birds eating the berries disperse the seeds. Ivy wood is very good for carving.

Ivy has great wildlife value. As ground cover in woodland, ivy greatly lessens the effect of frost, enabling birds and woodland creatures to forage in leaf litter during bitter spells. Growing on trees, it provides hiding, roosting, hibernating and nesting places for various animals, birds and insects (including butterflies), particularly during the winter months and in areas where there are few other evergreens.

Concept: Exchange

Ivy is not a parasite; its short, root-like growths which form the climbing stems are for support only; its own root system below ground supplies it with water and nutrients. It exchanges protection with the trees and ground for the support they give to the ivy. It offers food and protection to wildlife who, in turn, spread its seeds.

Gort, ivy, is also about exchange between thisworld and otherworld. It grows spirally, in the helix, as the spiral of life (including DNA) grows and its spiral growth links us to the goddess and the strong life-force pulsing from the earth.

12th Month – I: Iolo: *Yew* & P/B: Peith: *Guelder Rose*

I: Iolo: Yew
Iolo, yew, is the fifth and final feast of the goddess.
Time: Samhain
Watchwords: *I am the tomb to every hope*
Metal: Lead
Planet: Saturn
Concept: Death & rebirth
Iolo represents the letter **I**

Yew Trees

Yew, *Taxus baccata*, is the longest-lived of all British trees, some are thousands of years old. It holds great knowing, *kenning*, and wisdom.

The word yew comes from the Proto-Germanic *īwa* and the rune Eihwaz is associated with the yew. Some of its other names are *Ywen* (Welsh), *Lubhar* (Gaelic), *Ibar* (Old Irish), *Iur* (Irish), palm tree (Kent).

The soft needles lie flat on either side of the twig; they are dark green above and a yellow-grey green below. The bark is a wonderful red-purple and breaks up into shallow scales. The leaves are toxic and the seed inside the bright red yew-berries highly toxic. The flesh of the berries themselves is sweet; they were thrown as good-luck charms over newlyweds, offering their sweetness and the tree's longevity ... along with their poison if the seeds are eaten.

Yew timber is heavy but very elastic and traditionally used for longbows and spears. The "Clacton spear tip" is the oldest wooden artefact ever found in Britain; estimates of its age range from 300,000 to 450,000 years old. It was found in Clacton, Essex in 1911 by J. Hazzledine Warren. The wood is so hard that a yew fence post is said to outlive one made of iron. It's also used for domestic utensils and bowls, furniture, knife handles, cogs and wheels and parquet floors.

There are at least 500 churchyards in England which contain yew trees which are a lot older than the building itself. Yew trees are symbols of immortality. For many centuries it was the custom for yew branches to be carried on Palm Sunday and at funerals, hence the Kentish name.

Time: Samhain

Samhain is the turning of the year in the old British tradition, the time when the old year goes down to die and the new year is conceived ... not born yet, that happens at midwinter, but this is the time of the new year's conception.

In the not too distant past Samhain was the time when cattle were brought back down from the summer pastures and some were slaughtered for the winter meat which would be smoked to help it keep. Special protective and cleansing bonfires were lit and rituals done around them.

Samhain is one of the times when the boundaries between the spirit worlds and the everyday world are very thin; it is easy even for the unpractised to cross over ... and for spirit to visit with us. Feasts are made to which the souls of dead kin are beckoned and a place is set at the table for them; thus the ancestors are remembered.

This is a crucial time for the goddess, where she conceives the new year.

Watchwords

The watchwords for yew, iolo, are *I am the tomb of every hope*

A tomb is a place where things and/or people are laid after they are dead. Our ancestors used *ossuaries* and *charnel houses* to hold the relics, the bones, of their ancestors, the wise folk and the familiar animals. Bones can, as we know from archaeology, take many millions of years to decompose. The Christians picked up the habits of our ancestors when they began revering the bones, relics, of their saints as a link back to them.

So the tomb is a place to keep the links with the ancestors.

But what is hope and why is it entombed?

To hope is to have expectations, aspirations, wishes; it's often about designing the future to accord with our own wants ... and that doesn't have anything to do with asking the earth what she needs.

Hope is an odd, tricksy thing; it can turn very sour when we pin our faith on it but what is expected doesn't come to pass ... as we had hoped! We say *my hopes are dashed* and *there's no hope*. Long ago one of my teachers told me he went into every situation *"full of expectancy but without any expectations"*. He meant that he was open to anything that may come without pinning his own wants, expectations ... hopes ... on it. He left room for the universe to surprise him; he walked the universe's path rather than trying to constrict the universe into walking his own path. It was a marvellous gift to me, I pass it on.

Iolo helps us to learn to do this; to put aside our little personal hopes and make room for the big gifts the universe wants to offer us. The goddess, through iolo, will take these little personal desires and compost them for us, enabling them to go back into their constituent spirit-atoms so they can be remade into new life.

So, each year, we put our little personal hopes into the tomb iolo provides for us and come out, full of expectancy but without expectations, to find the new path. This is the death and rebirth feast we celebrate at this time of year.

Planet: Saturn

Saturn is about structure, bones, the skeleton that enables us not to be a blob!

Think about what your skeleton does, how you would be without it. It gives you *form*, makes you the shape that you are. It gives strong levers for the muscles to attach to so that you can move. Bones take hundreds of thousands, millions, of years to decompose – think of dinosaur bones – so they hold the structures of life, and of how life has formed itself, way back into history. This is our connection to the ancestors; it's part of what the ancestors do for us. We can learn from them if we wish.

Metal: Lead

Lead is a bright and silvery metal with a very slight shade of blue when it's dry. It is the metal alchemists transform into gold. Think about what this means. Both lead and gold are wonderful and important metals; don't go rejecting lead as a "base metal" with all the insulting modern connotations this rejection has! Lead can also be poison – like the seeds in the yew berries – when we use it in the wrong ways. Lead tells us a lot about how to work with things and how we can die when we don't ask but try to force Nature into our ways rather than living with Hers.

Concept: Birth – Death – Rebirth

Samhain has been a time of death and rebirth for millennia in the northern hemisphere.

Yew was both the coffin-maker's and the wedding tree for many ages. These ideas combine birth, death and rebirth. Old yew trees show us this. They will curve their branches down to the ground so they take root again … the tree re-births herself.

Our ancestors – and the wise and cunning folk I grew up with – had very different notions of birth and death to current modern ones. While they very likely hoped the process of death wouldn't hurt, they had none of the fears of this transition that most 21st century people have. They knew that death is a threshold and gateway to return to otherworld, recuperate, meet old friends and make new ones before setting out again on the voyage of discovery that is incarnation. We have largely lost all that now in our carefully controlled, scientifically boxed-up world. This little, controllable (or so we think) world-in-a-box is far too small to encompass all the reality our forebears *knew* in their bones.

Ponder on this …

When you are born into thisworld you die to otherworld.
When you die to thisworld you are born again into other-world.

When you die, everything you learn in that incarnation is uploaded into the "cloud space" of your soul group so it's available to everyone and everything. Your incarnation and the kenning you gained through it, increases the knowing, kenning, nous and wisdom for everything, including the universe itself.

When we are born, we may not remember all the past wisdom that's available through our *cloud* … the trick is to learn to access it again! Samhain is a good moment for asking iolo to help you with this. The veils between the worlds are thin at the dark-time Samhain; it's a good time for crossing in both directions … to learn and use all that otherworld offers us to get more access to our useful pasts.

The herbaceous plants demonstrate this so beautifully for us as they die down right back into the ground over the winter, giving all the stored goodness in their bodies back to Mother Earth and then, in the spring, they rise back up out of the soil. We need to follow their example and give back to the earth at this time. We can do this without actually giving our bodies back (unless it's our time) but by giving what we have made and grown, sharing with all of life, the animal, plant and mineral worlds as well as our fellow humans … uploading and downloading to our spirit-cloud space.

P: Peith: *Guelder Rose*

Time: 28 Oct – 24 Nov
Concept: Moon-blood
Peith represents our letter **P**

Here is where I differ radically from most known traditions. Most call this is the time of the reed but I use the guelder rose for this season. Scholarly arguments continue: I prefer to work with what I find by asking and journeying rather than the heady debates of scholars.

Guelder Rose

Guelder rose, *Viburnum opulus*, belongs to the same family as the elder and is often found in copses and hedgerows throughout England. However, it's rare in Scotland. It's also called snowball tree; king's crown; high cranberry; rose elder; water elder; May rose; Whitsun rose; whittan; dog rowan tree; silver bells; Whitsun bosses; gaitre berries (Chaucer's name for the tree) and black haw.

It's a deciduous shrub, which may grow five metres tall. In early summer its big, flat, multiple, cream/white, "lace-cap" flowerheads appear and are loved by many insects including hoverflies.

The fruits ripen very quickly, forming a drooping cluster of bright, shining and translucent red berries in August, against a background of rich purple autumn-coloured leaves. The berries are good food for birds, especially fieldfares and redwings, and used in jellies. In Siberia the berries are fermented with flour and a spirit distilled from them; in Norway and Sweden they use them to flavour a paste of honey and flour.

The berries have anti-scorbutic properties. They turn black in drying and have been used for making ink and a red dye can be made from the fruit while the wood, like that of the spindle tree and dogwood, is used for making skewers.

The bark, known as cramp bark, contains "scopolamine" which helps painful menstrual cramps and the fresh bark makes a homoeopathic remedy as a tonic for the heart and to relax cardiovascular muscles. Guelder-rose also treats swollen glands, asthma, colic, constipation and irritable bowel syndrome, as well as nervous tension, spasms of all kinds in convulsions, fits and lockjaw, and both leaves and fruits are laxative.

Concept: Moon-Blood

One of guelder rose's country names is "cramp bark" because it helps *menstrual* cramps. *Menses* is the Greek word for the woman's monthly blood-flow during her reproductive years and gives us the words menstruation and menstrual.

Samhain is the crone-time, the Old One, long past her menstrual years; now the *wise blood* no longer needs to flow each month but is turned into the poetry of lore. The red berries of the guelder rose give the crone the ink she needs to scribe her poetry, the ancestral wisdom.

The goddess' cycle is maiden, mother and crone. Inspiration from Upperworld rises within the maiden, feeding off the lorestories. The wise blood begins to flow at puberty so the woman may learn the wisdom of the Middleworld. When the wise blood ceases to flow she may become a wise crone, exploring deeply with the ancestors and bringing more of the lore to light. Guelder rose holds these qualities.

The Greek word *menses* has its root in *men* and is also a root of the word for month. The womb blood which nourishes the unborn child is known to have *"mana"* or "breath of life". The moon-blood, menstrual blood, that pours from women at the moon-time each month when there is no pregnancy for it to nourish, is given freely and was once used to nourish the tribe and the earth in other ways, e.g. composting.

A woman's bleeding is still considered by pagans as a vital part of life connecting us to the moon, the lunar cycles and the tides. A woman at this season is in a good time to listen to the moon-voice which will offer suggestions and wisdom that will benefit her whole tribe. It was only later, under patriarchal rule, that the moon-time was distorted into a perception of uncleanness. Women were forced to go apart, not allowed to participate in the preparation of food for men, or in ceremonies, and their wisdom denigrated, called lunacy and forced underground.

The advent of Christianity made this worse, the pendulum swung away from goddess-centred worship towards the patriarchal, man-centred place we are still largely in today. In Britain, this was exacerbated by the Norman Conquest which relegated women to being the *possessions* of fathers, brothers, husbands ... indeed just about any male! My recent ancestors headed the movement for the Married Women's Property Act without which women's' suffrage would not have happened, so I get quite passionate about this!

Peith, guelder rose, is a good time to contemplate the cycles of the goddess and the crossings between the worlds including your own time of passing from this incarnation back into otherworld, ready to train up for your next incarnation. Doing this will give you a very different perspective on life in general.

13th Month – R: Ruis: *Elder*

Time: 25 Nov – 23 Dec
Concept: Elder is the tree of *Enchantment*
Ruis represents our letter R

R: Ruis: Elder

Elder, *Sambucus nigra*, is a small bushy tree native to most of Europe. It likes sunny locations and will tolerate both wet and dry fertile soils.

Typically it is found with nettles on old dumps, where the soil is full of nitrogen. The elder roots spread out initially from a gnarled centre, checking for nutrients and, when found, grow downwards. New shoots can appear from any part of its trunk at any time. Elder grows equally well in banks and hedges (where it is excellent for layering), by rivers or in open woodland.

The flowers and inner bark are famous for their therapeutic qualities. The flowers make excellent wine and champagne. The berries are very good for a cordial that helps with winter colds as well as being a lovely drink in its own right.

Elder can be used to treat over 70 conditions; the bark can be good for "women's" conditions including promoting labour; it's also a good diuretic if used in small doses after being dried and powdered. The flower water eases sunburn; the berries make good wines, jams and teas.

Her name, elder, comes from the Anglo-Saxon word *aeld*: the tree was called eldrun. In Low-Saxon the name appears as ellhorn. *Ald* meant "fire," the hollow stems of the young branches having been used as blow-pokers for blowing up a fire. The soft pith pushes out easily and the tubes used as pipes, hence it was called pipe-tree, bore-tree and bour-tree which last name may still be heard in Scotland. She is called ysgawen in Welsh and Frau Holla in Germany.

She brings us back again to the ancient crone, the old wise face of the White Goddess. A guardian and protector of house and farm, she was offered cakes and milk in Scotland, milk in Sweden, and bread and beer in Germany. Elder wood is generally not cut down or burnt without good reason. Christianity attempted to poison the view of the elder, calling it "evil elder" and saying that Judas Iscariot hanged himself on an elder.

The Lady Ellhorn and Ellan are potent forms of the goddess, suggesting Elen of the Ways, the antlered goddess, the ancient one who stands behind all her other forms for the lands within the Boreal Forest.

Our ancestors – and I've seen this when I was growing up – always asked before cutting elder, "Lady Ellhorn, give me some of thy wood and I will give thee some of mine when it grows in the forest". Exchange, I will give you if you give me, an essential part of the British tradition.

There's a story from a Mr. Jones (quoted in THE TREASURY OF BOTANY), in his Notes on Certain Superstitions in the Vale of Gloucester, as follows:

Some men were employed in removing an old hedgerow, partially formed of Eldertrees. They had bound up all the other wood into faggots for burning, but had set apart the elder and enquired of their master how it was to be disposed of. Upon his saying that he should of course burn it with the rest, one of the men said with an air of undisguised alarm, that he had never heard of such a thing as burning Ellan Wood, and in fact, so strongly did he feel upon the subject, that he refused to participate in the act of tying it up. The word Ellan (still common with us) indicates the origin of the superstition.

Concept: En-chanting

Elder holds the season of sun-return, midwinter, and is about the magic of enchantment.

En-chant-ment is how we sing our spirits to life within us, how we sing our souls back home, how we walk between the worlds.

Elder is called the *pipe tree*. Its branches consist of an outer hard shell surrounding inner pith which can be pushed out, or left to dry out, leaving a hollow stem which makes a good pan-pipe. It's used in the Welsh bagpipes to make the "chanter" – the pibgorn as it's called, "gorn" meaning "horn".

Pipe music has been known as a means of enchantment for millennia. It offers a sound-gateway to journeying.

Mistletoe

Mistletoe, *Viscum album*, will grow on almost any deciduous tree but prefers those with soft bark and is commonest on old apple trees although it is frequently found on ash, hawthorn and lime. It very seldom grows on oak and so, when it does, is much treasured. Druids and others cunning folk find oak-grown mistletoe very powerful. Looking back to the qualities of the oak, and it being the British World Tree, this makes sense.

It is one of the major magical plants of Britain and sacred to many folks of the Boreal Forest.

Its name is said to come from the Anglo-Saxon *Misteltan, tan* signifying twig, and *mistel* from mist so meaning twig of mists. In the fourteenth century it was termed *Mystyldene*. Other names are all-heal, birdlime mistletoe, golden bough, Devil's euge and mistel.

It is a strange plant, having no roots in the soil but especially liking to live on the boughs of apple, qwert. Again, looking back on the qualities of apple and wisdom and we can see how the mistletoe draws these qualities, along with those of the oak, together in itself.

It attaches itself to the branch of the tree and penetrates it so that it can absorb water and nutrients from its host. It is a poisonous plant which causes acute gastrointestinal problems including stomach pain and diarrhoea along with low pulse if you eat it.

I know it from childhood teachings. We use its white berries as part of the midwinter feast along with the red of holly and the black of ivy ... the white, red and black, the three colours of the Celtic tradition.

Mistletoe's white berries are about the mother part of the goddess and about middleworld. Mistletoe hangs on the boughs of the tree, only rooted in earth through the tree that supports it.

It hangs in the middle, connected to the earth and the sky through the tree of wisdom. It is very common in Herefordshire, where I live now and I still collect it regularly every midwinter to decorate the house.

These three colours, red, white and black, are the colours that hold the essence of the three worlds for the British and Celtic tradition.

Red, White, Black

The red, white and black of the Celtic tradition are ...

Here's an idea of the correspondences ...

RED	WHITE	BLACK
Holly	**Mistletoe**	**Ivy**
Red Cup of Lordship	White Cup of Fostering	Black Cup of Forgetfulness
Red Book of Hergest	White Book of Rhydderch	Black Book of Carmarthen
Upperworld	Thisworld	Lowerworld
Maiden	Mother	Crone
Blacksmith	Healer	Poet
Upperworld	Middleworld	Lowerworld
Inspiration	Love	Wisdom

These hold the fundamental energies of the British way; Frayde (the Brythonic name for Brighid) holds them in her three faces of Blacksmith, Healer and Poet. We use the berries of the three trees – holly, mistletoe and ivy – in our midwinter and sun-return celebrations.

- Mistletoe holds the healer and fostering energy of the mother and Middleworld.
- Holly holds the inspirational energy of the maiden and Upperworld.

- Ivy holds the ancestral wisdom-energy of the crone and Lowerworld

Ways to work with the Trees

Background Reading ...
Robert Graves – THE WHITE GODDESS
Sir James Fraser – THE GOLDEN BOUGH

Jottings and Drawings and Scribblings ...

The work is about *making connections* and expanding our kenning, our *knowing* rather than our *knowledge*. Scribbles, drawing, and jotting are really good for this.

Get yourself a special book in which you can play, keep your own drawings and notes of what happens as you work through the year of the trees. This isn't like a school homework book, it doesn't have to be neat and tidy, in fact it's much better and more useful if it isn't. Working creatively like this allows your intuition and feelings to work, rather than just your intellect. You're going to *play* with the work and with the trees, and their spirits. They will take you places, tell and show you things you never even dreamed of ... it's fun!

Sit-With

This is a vital listening skill that will help you work with the trees of the goddess. You can use it for anything. It's about learning to *listen* and to *hear* with an open mind, *not* jumping to conclusions or making assumptions. It's about hearing what was actually told you rather than translating it into what you think was meant.

Have a go at the following ...

Take a word, any noun will do, and write it down on a clean sheet of paper.

Sit quiet with your word, *give it your full attention*, as if it was your best beloved – for so it is.

Give yourself *no more than* 10 minutes.

Jot down *images, words and/or phrases* which come into your mind. These will be from the word itself, *if* you are giving it your full attention.

Do *not* try to understand or make sense, just listen, see pictures, feel.

No "stream of consciousness" stuff either, just brief, succinct words/phrases.

You may only get one or two images/words/phrases, that's fine.

Stop at 10 minutes, or before if you feel the off switch go – get used to knowing when your own personal *on/off-switch* happens. Do *not* extend the time.

Have a cup of tea, put the whole thing out of your conscious mind. This is very important!

Don't worry at it like a terrier with a bone; that clogs up your unconscious so it can't work properly

When you've finished your tea, go back and *look at* (don't read! just look) at the images, words and phrases which came to you. *Absorb* them.

Again, *don't* try to make sense, allow *digestion* and *incubation* to take place.

Every now and then over the next few days go and look at the paper again, stir the pot so to speak. The cauldron-pot of your unconscious will continue to boil and bubble and new drops of inspiration will leap out at you every now and again, probably when you least expect it.

As you gain more experience and ability with this technique you can extend this exercise to asking about the images and words you got from the original exercise. Do it as often as you can, it will help you learn to listen.

Listening in the way is NOT about interpreting. You don't use your mind to "work things out" or "understand" … you allow the word/image to show you what it is about.

This helps you gain confidence in knowing the difference between when you are hearing spirit and when your mind is taking control and giving you a load of rubbish. Most people starting on this path worry about kidding themselves ... this exercise helps you to learn the difference.

Moon Bath

Sit out in the path of the full moon (you don't need to be naked for this!) Feel the moonlight wash over you and through you.

Remember what moonlight is ... the *reflected* light of the sun. At the time of the full moon the moon and sun stand directly opposite each other, like dancers in a country dance. Between them is the earth ... and you. The moon takes and changes the quality of the sun's light, and then reflects it down onto the earth (and you) ... Sense into this quality.

Try to let go of all the preconceptions you've read about what the moon signifies. Ask the moon to help you wash yourself clean of these preconceptions so you can hear what she has to tell and show you rather than be all cluttered up with the things other humans have written.

As one of my teachers used to say – *be full of expectancy but with no expectations.*

Listen to the moon; watch what she shows and tells you.

Solstice Work – Stand Still

The word solstice means *standstill*. At the solstice the sun appears stand still for three days. This means it seems to rise in the same place on the horizon for 3 days. Then, after the 3 days, it moves on again to rise in a different place on the horizon each day.

For the 3 days of the solstice make time for yourself to STAND STILL each day.

- The winter solstice days are the 22nd, 23rd and 24th December
- The summer solstice days are 22nd, 23rd and 24th June

This is the death and rebirth of the sun which our ancestors celebrated at places like Maen Howe, Skara Brae, Stonehenge and many less well-known sacred places in our land.

Each solstice spend the 3 days of standstill standing still. This is a time to thank and let go of the past so making space to open yourself up to the future. This *letting go* is part of what the time of the solstices is about.

Say these words at the beginning of each your three standstill days …

I thank everything that has brought me to this now this time and place of my life, and I let it go.

At the end of each your standstill days say these words …

I open myself to the new good which is waiting to come into me.

Make notes and drawings of what comes to you on each of the 3 days. Ponder over your findings over the time after the solstice and ask that you may see you next step forward.

Equinox Work – Balance

The two sun-feasts of the spring and autumn equinoxes are times of balance.

Only on these 2 days does the sun rise in the due east and set in the due west. All the other 363 days of the year the sun rises and sets either to the south or north of each of these points. From midwinter to midsummer the sun rises north of east and sets north of west; so our days get longer and our nights shorter. From midsummer to midwinter the sun rises south east and sets south of west; so our days get shorter and the nights longer.

Make space-time for yourself at sunrise and sunset on each of the equinoxes.

Stand in place where you can see the sun as it rises over and goes down below the horizon in the evening. The seashore is particularly good for this but unless you are on a very small island it's not going to be possible as you won't be able to see both sunrise and sunset! A high open place is very good and far more possible; and you are likely to be able to stay there all day. This a very good idea; you can spend time, spend the day, with the spirit of earth and with your spirit allies.

Say these words at each equinox sunrise and sunset, at your balance-place ...

At the still point of the turning world. Neither flesh nor fleshless;
Neither from nor towards; at the still point, there the dance is,
But neither arrest nor movement.
And do not call it fixity,
Where past and future are gathered. Neither movement from nor
towards,
Neither ascent nor decline. Except for the point, the still point,
There would be no dance, and there is only the dance.

These words come from TS Eliot's poem Burnt Norton (from his FOUR QUARTETS).

Ponder on them. Eliot's poem gives the real feel for the balance point and his phrases ... *there the dance is ... and there is only the dance.*

Standing at the still point enables you to experience the dance.

Allies ...

Allies are our companions and teachers in this work. This section is about journeying; on the journey you meet and befriend the tree-allies, the spirits of the ogham trees.

Trees are whole worlds in themselves and they will show and tell us so much if we ask. They are homes and food for many other creatures. They make oxygen for other creatures to breathe (including us). They absorb carbon dioxide to keep the planet at the temperature she needs to be for all the creatures who live on her. They help make clouds, water, through temperature changes brought about by lots of them growing together in a forest. Go and look up all the things trees do; these are the beings you are asking to work with.

Journey

This technique is safe and respectful of otherworld – being respectful is the best way of being safe!

Clean the space, make it nice.

Have ...

- A candle to remind you of fire;
- Some flowers to remind you of the scent of air;
- A little pot of the soil where you live to remind you of earth;
- A pot of water from your tap to remind you of the water you use every day.

Make sure you won't be interrupted for about an hour; turn off your phone; tell your family/friends to leave you alone for that time.

Have ...

- Water to drink,
- Tissues in case you need them,
- Paper and coloured pens to record things,
- A clock to check the time,
- A recording of drumming

Lie down, make yourself comfortable and close/cover your eyes. Now, lie still.

Feel your breathing. Don't try to change anything. Feel yourself lying comfortably and safely under your blanket. *Know* that you are in your own sacred space.

Say your purpose out loud, 3 times. *I am here to meet the spirit of ... [say the name of the tree you are working with]*

Now wait. The spirit *will* come to you.

Invite the spirit into your sacred space.

Ask the spirit to *show* you about itself.

Ask the spirit what it needs you to do for it.

This is about *making friends with* the spirit.

You will make exchanges with the spirit ... When you work with otherworld there is always exchange ... you give to them and they give to you.

Begin by ASKING what you may do for the spirit.

Don't set off with a shopping list of your own wants! Ask the spirit what it needs. Later in the journey the spirit will offer you something – this will be something that you need.

Go with the spirit; see and hear what it has to show and tell you.

When you and the spirit have done enough for the day, *thank the spirit* for all it has given you and ask it to be there with you when you return from the journey while you learn more about its tree; and to be with you while you make its stave.

You also need thank the sacred space for containing you and

holding you.

When you are ready, gently come back to the everyday world.

Turn on one side and curl up in the foetal position for a few minutes. Gently recall, in your mind's eye, where you have been ... remember your journey. Begin to digest what you have learned.

You need now to reclaim your body, get to know and feel it again after you have been journeying out of it for half an hour. You need to greet your body and thank it for still being there for you to come back to – don't take it for granted!

When you are ready, gently sit up and then get up.

Make drawings and notes; use colour as it really helps and is much better than trying to write grammatical English.

Now you need to eat and drink to replace the physical energy you have used and to anchor yourself in your body again; Journeying is hard work on the body even if it looks like you're just lying there!

Now, clear your space; don't leave bits of your journey hanging about like old cobwebs.

Making your Ogham Staves

Finding the Wood

To find the wood you ASK the spirit to help you find what it needs to make its stave.

As you go looking, hold this request in your mind ... *"Please lead me to the wood for your ogham stave."* The form of this request is important! You *ask* the spirit to guide you. You don't use your head, don't think, don't try to work it out for yourself ... you ask and listen.

When the spirit shows you the wood it needs, *ask the tree* if you may take/cut the wood.

This way of working, asking and listening, helps you learn to *work with* everything. You never take a twig or branch from a tree without asking, without the agreement of the spirit that is giving a part of its life, be this tree, flower, carrot, insect or animal – or human. There is always commitment to the contract of life-exchange. And ... you *always give back* in some way for what you take. You gift the tree in return for what it has given to you when you take the branch that the tree-spirit offers you to make its spirit-home – this is exchange.

Making the Stave

Making the stave is to *make a spirit-house,* a body, for the spirit to inhabit. This is a wonderful, magical thing to do. It will use all your skills of asking, listening, sitting-with, not knowing best and allowing spirit to lead your hands. This is being open to the needs of otherworld.

The end result, the stave, will surprise you. Even if you've always felt you can't do craft work you'll find that the stave you make, with the help of the tree spirit, will be far more than you had imagined.

There's no need to make the staves like others you may

already have seen. Be open! Remember ... be full of expectancy but with no expectations. Listen to what the tree spirit wants; ask the spirit to show you what it wants and needs, don't impose your ideas on it.

Embodying Ritual ...

When the stave is made the spirit will ask to be *embodied* in it. This is a very magical act. The following is a simple and safe way of doing this, both for the spirit and for you.

Embodying and **enlivening** is about magic. You will find doing this changes and enlarges your whole life. It will expand all your relationships, making everything more alive both within you and all around you. In turn, your new aliveness will enable others. It's a magic spiral that enables growth.

Go over this procedure a few times beforehand, so you've an idea of what you'll be doing.

You will need to sit up for this ...

- Prepare the space as you do for journeying.
- Take the ogham stave in your hands.
- Find yourself within your sacred space.
- Invite the ogham spirit to join you there.
- Show the ogham spirit the spirit-home you have made.
- Say *"The house is made and ready, please come to live there, I will care for you and work with you"*.
  - Never seek to hold or trap the spirit within the wood! It is completely the spirit's choice whether it stays there or comes and goes.
- See/feel the spark go out from your heart and into the stave in your hands. This may give you a rush.
- You will know by the change in physical sensation when it is done.
- When that moment comes, thank the spirit.
- Close the space as you do when journeying.

- Put the stave in its own place, with the others as you come to make them all. They may want a bag or box of their own ... *ask them* what they would like, it's another spirit-house for you to make ...

Now, get yourself something to drink and eat ... you've worked hard and need to replenish your physical body for carrying some quite high-powered cosmic-current through it successfully.

Use this ritual to embody each of the ogham staves.

Spirit Keeping

A spirit keeper is a guardian and helper ... one who *works with* the spirits ... taking care of them and of their place on earth, in the environment. The spirit keeper also has the job of passing on this knowing, *kenning*, so that others may know spirit too.

As a spirit-keeper – we call it being *awenydd*, being a shaman, in Britain – I feel wholly connected to both the spirit and the physical world; we call this *walking between worlds*. As I write, early of a summer's morning, a lark wings her way sunward in a cloud of song; the poplars outside my window whisper their leaves with the light breeze; the roses send their scent through the open window. All these are things of spirit just as much as they are part of the physical world. All of life, mineral, plant and animal has spirit and that includes me and you ... and the trees.

This book is about how we work with our British sacred trees to enlarge our knowing, our *kenning*, of the universe. We make friends with the tree spirits. We get to know them physically – their roots, trunks, branches, leaves, flowers and fruits – and their spirits.

In Britain we call the wisdom of the trees the ogham. Academe says the ogham is an Early Medieval alphabet primarily used to write the Old Irish and the Brythonic languages, and let's not open the can of worms that is the Norse ogham! Ogham is sometimes called the Celtic Tree Alphabet and based on a medieval tradition ascribing names of trees to the individual letters. There are roughly 400 surviving ogham inscriptions on stone monuments throughout Ireland and western Britain the bulk of which are in the south of Ireland. The largest number outside of Ireland is in Pembrokeshire in Wales; the rest are in Scotland, Orkney, the Isle of Man, and around the Devon/Cornwall border in England.

Ogham has a mixed, muddled and cluttered academic history.

The earliest known ogham inscriptions are on stone and date from about the 4th century AD. Current academic wisdom says it was invented by the Irish at about that time. The Irish scholar James Carney believes differently and says it was invented sometime in the 1st century BC. If you read the much maligned and academically discredited Robert Graves you get a different story again. It seems that nobody really knows. Whatever its origins this book is about *working with* the trees and their spirits as a spirit-keeper rather than arguing its academic history.

Enjoy your exploration of the trees of the goddess.

Moon Books invites you to begin or deepen your encounter with
Paganism, in all its rich, creative, flourishing forms.